Best BIBLE Bits

Best BIBLE Bits

Compiled by

The pupils of Greenway Boys'
Comprehensive School, Bristol

with

Janet Green

Design

Bill Bruce

CIO PUBLISHING
Church House, Dean's Yard, Westminster, London SW1P 3NZ

ISBN 0 7151 0420 9

Published 1984 for the General Synod Board of Education
by CIO Publishing

Contents

New Testament:

Foreword

Many schools did projects about the Bible during 'The Year of the Bible'. At Greenway Secondary School, a boys' comprehensive in Bristol, we took part in the Three Counties Bible Project organised by Dorothy Jamal, the Diocesan R.E. Adviser for Bath and Wells/Bristol.

We started off conventionally by finding out about the Bible: how it was written, how it came to us and the difficulties some people in the world still experience trying to obtain a copy.

We became interested in the different responses of people to the Bible. Some boys did a street survey (see page 79). But it seemed tame stuff after the experience of compiling the words and photographs for our book **Home Made Prayers** which had just been published by Lion.

There were a few enthusiastic pupils who had been checking Bible word puzzles for **Harlequinade** (by Janet Green, published by CIO Publishing). I asked them how they would encourage other teenagers to look at a Bible.

One boy suggested writing to famous people to ask which bit of the Bible they liked best.

'If their hero reads the Bible they might look at it.'
'What if their hero doesn't read the Bible?'
'Well, that'll be interesting to find out too.'

A few volunteers began writing to people of their choice. We had intended compiling a list of forty famous people. I was interested to see whom the kids would choose so I took no part in making the selection.

A letter to Prince Charles went out first but, without waiting to see if we'd get a reply, the volunteers continued writing. Very quickly enthusiasm spread throughout the school. Every class joined in – from first years to fifth years. About 200 boys have taken part. We are a small school, due for closure (which will, sadly, have taken place by the time you read this), so in fact this number represents the majority of the pupils. We soon passed our limit of forty famous people too.

The letters were written in the boys' spare time: before and after school, in break times and at home. Some children with writing difficulties were helped by older boys and even by parents and girlfriends. I didn't correct the letters unless they were totally baffling. In those cases I added a postscript of explanation.

Some boys took it upon themselves to help locate addresses and gave up spare time to go to town to the main reference library. Some of them had never been in a library before. For me it was a very rewarding moment when I wandered into the central library and happened upon a group of them. Skinheads, bother boots and tomes of **Who's Who** make a strange combination.

The addresses were proving to be the main problem. Those given in pop magazines seemed to draw a total blank. We wrote to more pop stars than any other section of people but had a reply from only one, Cliff Richard. But then, as one boy said, 'You'd expect him to, wouldn't you. He's summat to do with God, isn't 'e?'

The Bristol Hippodrome had a pantomime starring most of the **Hi-de-Hi** cast and the boys were quick off the mark to write to them. Some took to reading the papers, listening out for addresses on radio and television or finding functions that famous people might be attending. That's how we contacted Roger Moore when he was filming **Octopussy**. We are also indebted to **Scene**, the programme produced by B.B.C. Schools' Television, for helping us to locate people in the entertainment world, and to Harry Carpenter, who has forwarded letters to sports personalities.

My contribution is to make sure that an up-to-date file is kept of letters sent and replies received. Photostats are made of everything, with the willing help of our Resources lady, Mrs Wright. The school secretaries, Mrs Harman and Mrs Daley, are our post office. The boys open their own replies and retain a photostat. They will receive the originals when the project is complete.

There is jubilation when a reply is received. The Headmaster, staff, caretakers and cleaning ladies show as much enthusiasm as the lads and speculation goes on 'reading between the lines' of the replies.

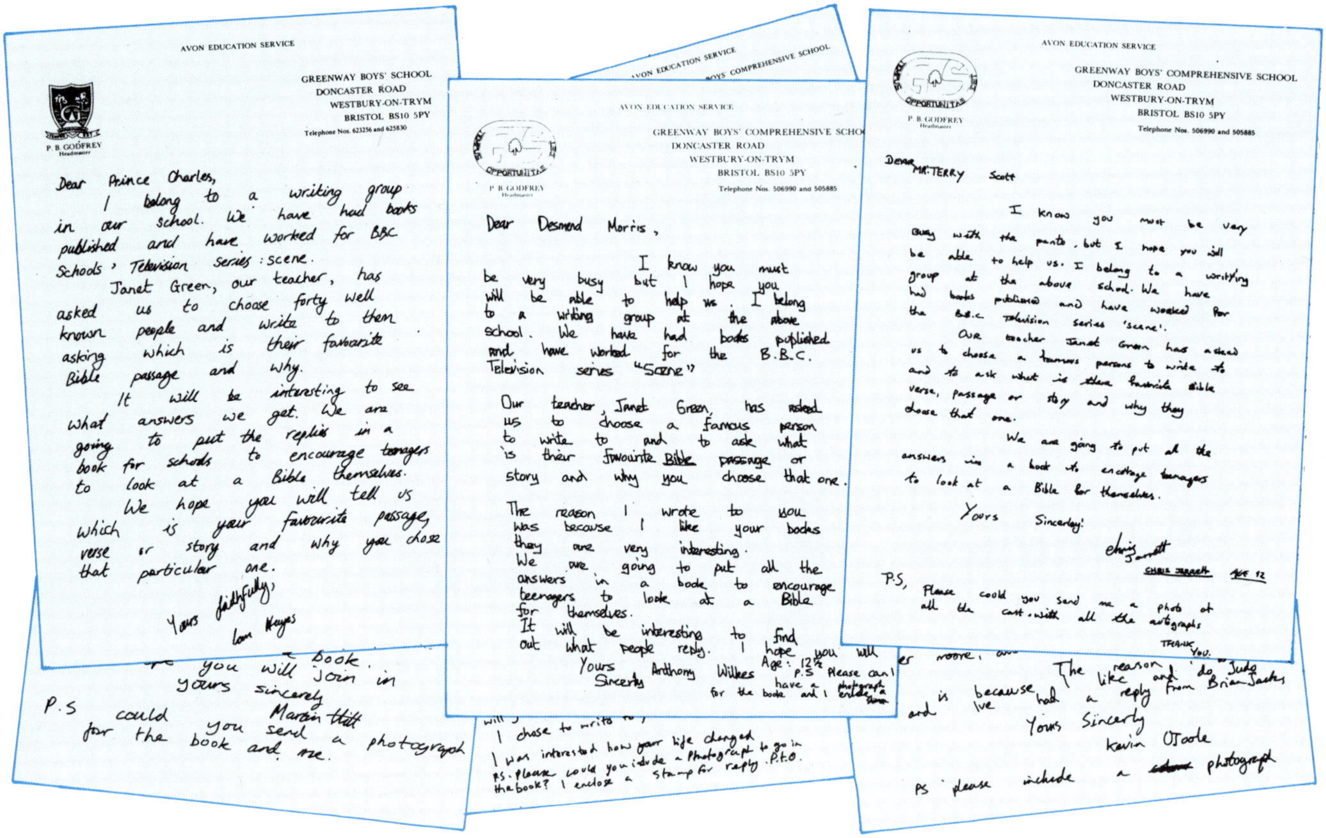
AVON EDUCATION SERVICE

GREENWAY BOYS' SCHOOL
DONCASTER ROAD
WESTBURY-ON-TRYM
BRISTOL BS10 5PY
Telephone Nos. 623256 and 625830

P. B. GODFREY
Headmaster

Dear Prince Charles,
I belong to a writing group in our school. We have had books published and have worked for BBC Schools' Television series: scene.
Janet Green, our teacher, has asked us to choose forty well known people and write to them asking which is their favourite Bible passage and why.
It will be interesting to see what answers we get. We are going to put the replies in a book for schools to encourage teenagers to look at a Bible themselves.
We hope you will tell us which is your favourite passage, verse or story and why you chose that particular one.
Yours faithfully,
Ian Hayes

... book. ... you will join in
yours sincerely
Martin Hill
P.S could you send a photograph for the book and me.

AVON EDUCATION SERVICE
GREENWAY BOYS' COMPREHENSIVE SCHOOL

AVON EDUCATION SERVICE

GREENWAY BOYS' COMPREHENSIVE SCHOOL
DONCASTER ROAD
WESTBURY-ON-TRYM
BRISTOL BS10 5PY
Telephone Nos. 506990 and 505885

OPPORTUNITAS
P. B. GODFREY
Headmaster

Dear Desmond Morris,
I know you must be very busy but I hope you will be able to help us. I belong to a writing group at the above school. We have had books published and have worked for the B.B.C. Television series "Scene"
Our teacher, Janet Green, has asked us to choose a famous person to write to and to ask what is their favourite Bible passage or story and why you choose that one.
The reason I wrote to you was because I like your books they are very interesting.
We are going to put all the answers in a book to encourage teenagers to look at a Bible for themselves.
It will be interesting to find out what people reply. I hope you will
Yours Sincerely Anthony Wilkes Age: 12½
P.S Please can I have a photograph for the book and I enclose a stamp

I chose to write to ...
I was interested how your life changed
P.S. please could you include a Photograph to go in the book? I enclose a stamp for reply. P.T.O.

AVON EDUCATION SERVICE

GREENWAY BOYS' COMPREHENSIVE SCHOOL
DONCASTER ROAD
WESTBURY-ON-TRYM
BRISTOL BS10 5PY
Telephone Nos. 506990 and 505885

OPPORTUNITAS
P. B. GODFREY
Headmaster

Dear MR. TERRY Scott
I know you must be very busy with the panto, but I hope you will be able to help us. I belong to a writing group at the above school. We have had books published and have worked for the B.B.C Television series 'scene'.
Our teacher Janet Green has asked us to choose a famous persons to write to and to ask what is there favorite bible verse, passage or story and why they chose that one.
We are going to put all the answers in a book to encourage teenagers to look at a Bible for themselves.
Yours Sincerley!
chris Jarrett
CHRIS JARRETT AGE 12
P.S, Please could you send me a photo of all the cast with all the autographs
THANK YOU.

... moore, ...
The reason is because I like and do Judo and I've had a reply from Brian Jacks
Yours Sincerly
Kevin O'Toole
PS please include a photograph

Hilarious Moments

There have been hilarious moments, such as the time when the boys, opening two letters which had come by the same post, confused the photo of Benny Hill and the letter from the Pope. 'I always wondered what he looked like without all his gear,' said one of them.

The Pope's reply was disappointing in that he didn't name a verse though, as one boy kindly observed, 'He can't choose just one, can he? He's the Pope. He's got to like them all.' We all agreed that the letter from the Vatican was the poshest we received. The paper has a marvellous eagle design in the watermark. One lad commented that he bet Jesus didn't have writing paper like that.

We wondered if there was a general Church policy involved in dealing with requests such as ours, when Cardinal Hume's reply was so similar to that which we received from the Pope. The boys had been keen to write to Cardinal Hume after seeing him on television during the Pope's visit to England. They had been impressed by the Cardinal's humility. That wasn't the phrase they used. The actual phrase was, 'he didn't seem bugged by having to take a back seat.'

We haven't written to many Church dignitaries simply because the children don't seem to think of writing to religious leaders. I was tempted to prompt them but I kept to my original decision not to influence their choice.

I was surprised when they decided to write to the Chief Rabbi and pleased when they realised he would only use the Old Testament.

In our school there are a few devout Muslims, Hindus and Christians but the majority of the pupils have no deep religious convictions. We often discuss the possible religious inclinations of people to whom they are writing. I find myself

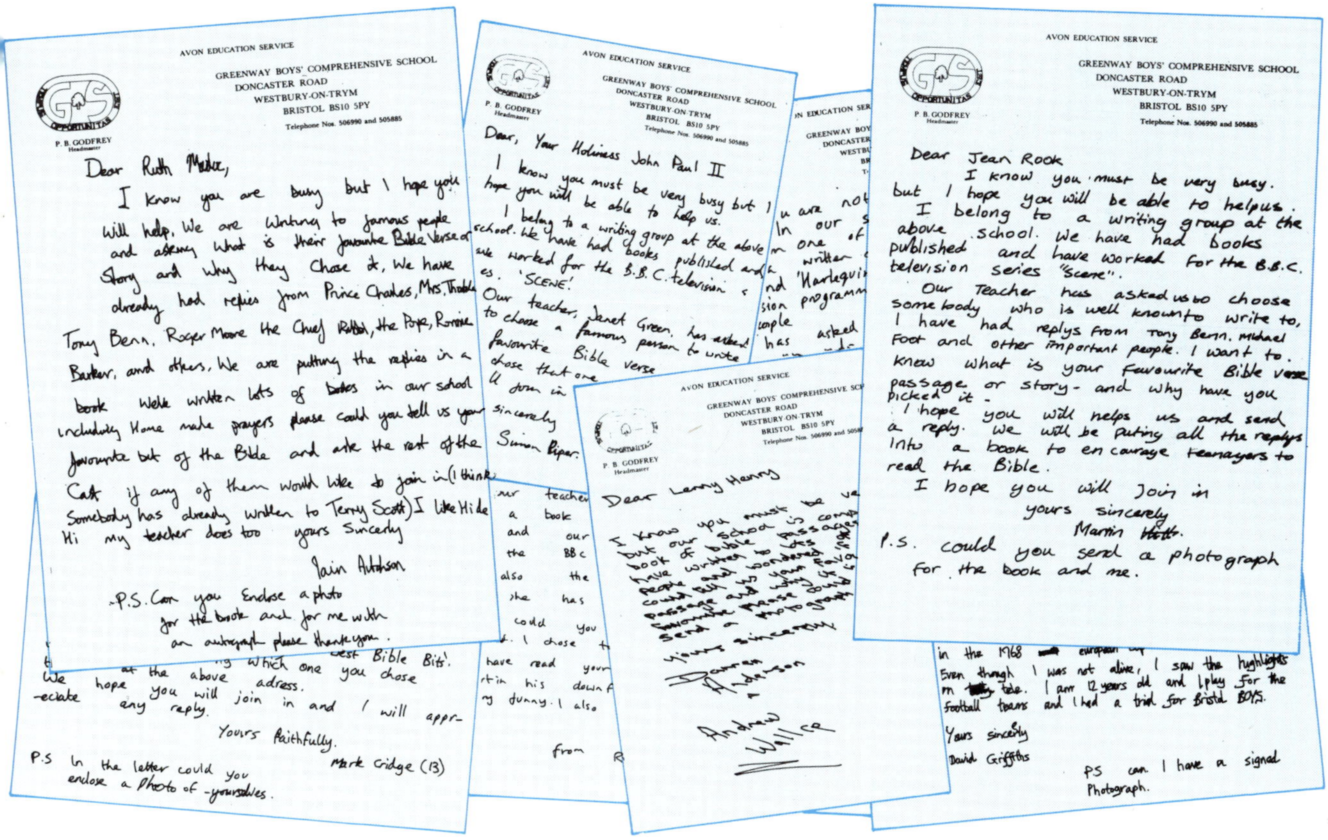

AVON EDUCATION SERVICE
GREENWAY BOYS' COMPREHENSIVE SCHOOL
DONCASTER ROAD
WESTBURY-ON-TRYM
BRISTOL BS10 5PY
Telephone Nos. 506990 and 505885
P. B. GODFREY, Headmaster

Dear Ruth Madoc,

I know you are busy but I hope you will help. We are writing to famous people and asking what is their favourite Bible Verse or Story and why they chose it, We have already had replies from Prince Charles, Mrs. Thatcher, Tony Benn, Roger Moore the Chief Rabbi, the Pope, Ronnie Barker, and others, We are putting the replies in a book. We've written lots of books in our school including Home made prayers please could you tell us your favourite bit of the Bible and ask the rest of the Cast if any of them would like to join in (I think somebody has already written to Terry Scott) I like Hi de Hi my teacher does too yours Sincerely

Iain Aitchison

P.S. Can you Enclose a photo for the book and for me with an autograph please thank you.

AVON EDUCATION SERVICE
GREENWAY BOYS' COMPREHENSIVE SCHOOL
DONCASTER ROAD
WESTBURY-ON-TRYM
BRISTOL BS10 5PY
Telephone Nos. 506990 and 505885
P. B. GODFREY, Headmaster

Dear Jean Rook

I know you must be very busy. but I hope you will be able to helpus. I belong to a writing group at the above school. We have had books published and have worked for the B.B.C. television series "Scene".

Our Teacher has asked us to choose somebody who is well known to write to, I have had replys from Tony Benn, Michael Foot and other important people. I want to know what is your Favourite Bible verse passage or story - and why have you picked it -

I hope you will helps us and send a reply. We will be puting all the replys into a book to en courage teenagers to read the Bible.

I hope you will Join in

yours sincerely
Martin

P.S. could you send a photograph for the book and me.

frequently answering very sincere questions about beliefs and practices of Christian denominations, of other world faiths and of more secular life stances. We were interested to receive the replies of David Attenborough and Desmond Morris because the boys had correctly anticipated the style of response. Much fruitful discussion followed.

The entertainment world – comedians and television stars – seems to be full of individuals who share the sentiments which I call 'folk religion and grass roots Christianity'. I found this aspect of faith was alive and well among our boys and their families when we collected **Home Made Prayers**, and this present book has convinced me of the strength of these beliefs in our society at large.

The letter-writing experience has involved us in other discussions besides those on religion. Replies following a 'too busy to answer in person' formula provoked much thought about celebrities. Were they annoyed when the public intruded on their lives or should they expect this? What obligations have celebrities to their fans?

We weren't surprised that our most prompt replies usually came from politicians. Tony Benn was among the first and his reply was handwritten. It provoked the lovely response, 'Look, Miss, he writes joined up!' He also returned the stamp we had sent and this small touch impressed the boys. They noted his greeting to me and said, 'You have to give him this; he does his homework.'

Michael Foot had referred to the Gospel of Hope, and that set them looking in the Bible for a book of that name! Mrs Thatcher's reply provoked long discussions on politics and religion. I was staggered to find the boys using concepts like 'the establishment'. Curiously, nobody has suggested writing to any SDP leaders.

The younger boys are frequently confused between television roles and real characters. They also find it hard to accept that some actors they see on the screen

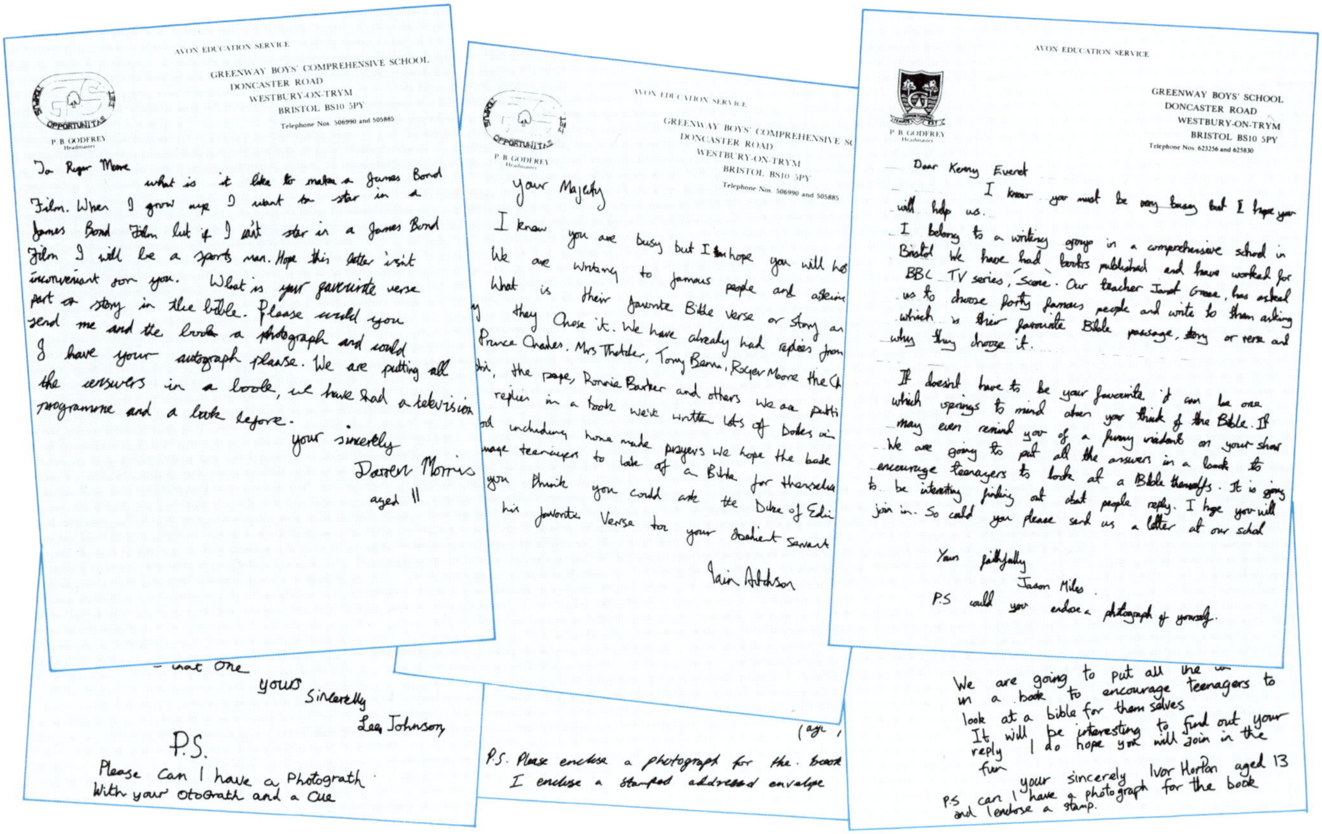
AVON EDUCATION SERVICE
GREENWAY BOYS' COMPREHENSIVE SCHOOL
DONCASTER ROAD
WESTBURY-ON-TRYM
BRISTOL BS10 5PY
Telephone Nos. 506990 and 505885
P. B. GODFREY
Headmaster

To Roger Moore
what is it like to make a James Bond Film. When I grow up I want to star in a James Bond Film but if I can't star in a James Bond Film I will be a sports man. Hope this letter isn't inconvenient for you. What is your favourite verse part or story in the bible. Please would you send me and the book a photograph and could I have your autograph please. We are putting all the answers in a book, we have had a television programme and a book before.
your sincerely
Darren Morris
aged 11

AVON EDUCATION SERVICE
GREENWAY BOYS' COMPREHENSIVE SC
DONCASTER ROAD
WESTBURY-ON-TRYM
BRISTOL BS10 5PY
Telephone Nos. 506990 and 505885
P. B. GODFREY
Headmaster

Your Majesty
I know you are busy but I hope you will he
We are writing to famous people and askin
What is their favorite Bible verse or story an
y they chose it. We have already had replies from
Prince Charles. Mrs Thatcher, Tony Benn, Roger Moore the C
hi, the pope, Ronnie Barker and others we are putti
replies in a book we've written lots of books in
nd including home made prayers we hope the book
urage teenagers to take of a Bible for themselve
you think you could ask the Duke of Edi
his favorite Verse for your obedient servant
Iain Aitchison

AVON EDUCATION SERVICE
GREENWAY BOYS' SCHOOL
DONCASTER ROAD
WESTBURY-ON-TRYM
BRISTOL BS10 5PY
Telephone Nos. 623256 and 625830
P. B. GODFREY
Headmaster

Dear Kenny Everett
I know you must be very busy but I hope you will help us.
I belong to a writing group in a comprehensive school in Bristol We have had books published and have worked for BBC TV series, 'Score'. Our teacher Janet Green, has asked us to choose forty famous people and write to them asking which is their favourite Bible passage, story or verse and why they choose it.
It doesn't have to be your favourite it can be one which springs to mind when you think of the Bible. It may even remind you of a funny incident on your show
We are going to put all the answers in a book to encourage teenagers to look at a Bible themselfs. It is going to be interesting finding out what people reply. I hope you will join in. So could you please send us a letter at our school
Yours faithfully
Jason Miles
P.S could you enclose a photograph of yourself.

– that one
yours Sincerelly
Lee Johnson
P.S.
Please can I have a Photograth
With your otoGrath and a Cue

(age
P.S. Please enclose a photograph for the book
I enclose a stamped addressed envelope

We are going to put all the in a book to encourage teenagers to look at a bible for them selves
It will be interesting to find out your reply I do hope you will join in the fun
your sincerely Ivor Horton aged 13
P.S can I have a photograph for the book and I enclose a stamp.

are actually dead. One boy went into the sulks for days because he couldn't write to John Wayne and treated me as if it were my fault!

A boy in 1C wrote to Ronnie Corbett. Every day the lad waited for me in the corridor and asked if there was a reply. I grew as anxious as he was. Then one day, he wasn't waiting; he was late for school. It was the very day the reply arrived. The first the boy knew about it was when the Headmaster summoned him on to the stage in Assembly to receive the letter. I'll never forget that moment; his little face positively beaming, he actually skipped all the way.

I still smile when I see the photostat of the letter to Ernest Borgnine: 'Can I have a photo of you. Here is a photo of me. You can keep it.' I have explained to writers such as this one that it will take months to get replies from overseas, but it hasn't deterred them from continuing to write. Letters are on their way to the Kremlin, the Aga Khan, Uri Geller, Lech Walesa and numerous Hollywood stars.

For many boys it was the first time they had stopped to think which television series are local, which national, which British and which American. They are often surprised to find that some apparently new series were actually made decades ago. For some boys it is the first time they have written a real letter and for many the first time they have received one.

Different Bibles

Bibles became well thumbed as the lads looked up the context of each reply. Then we decided how much of a passage to use in the book. There is no doubt in our minds that the Authorized Version is still well loved and the one that is

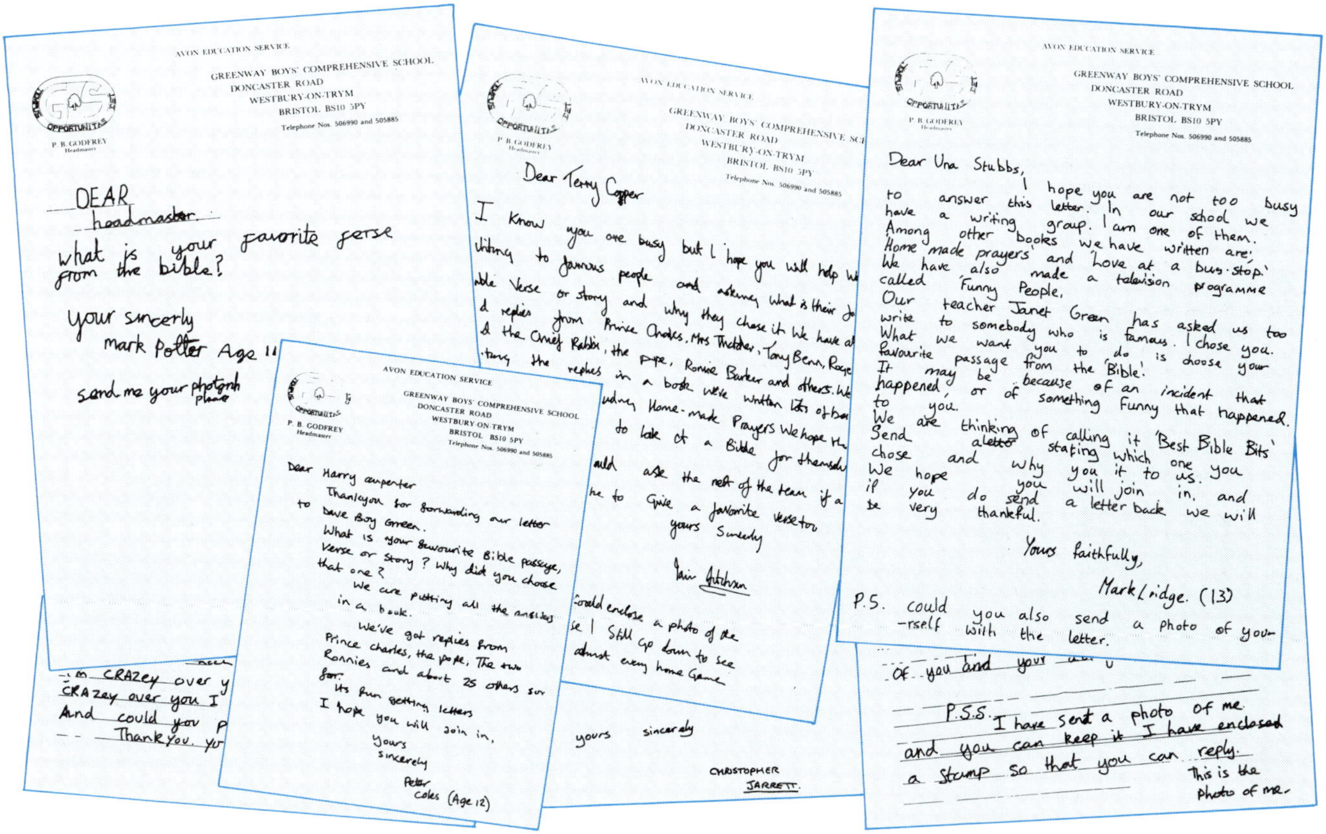

AVON EDUCATION SERVICE
GREENWAY BOYS' COMPREHENSIVE SCHOOL
DONCASTER ROAD
WESTBURY-ON-TRYM
BRISTOL BS10 5PY
Telephone Nos. 506990 and 505885
P. B. GODFREY
Headmaster

DEAR headmaster
what is your favorite ferse from the bible?
your sincerly
mark Potter Age 11
send me your photograph please

Dear Terry Cooper
I know you are busy but I hope you will help ... writing to famous people and asking what is their ... ble Verse or story and why they chose it. We have al... d replies from Prince Charles, Mrs Thatcher, Tony Benn, Ro... d the Chief Rabbi, the pope, Ronnie Barker and others. We ... in a book. ... Home-made Prayers. We hope ... to look at a Bible for themselv... ask the rest of the team if a... to Give a favourite verse too
yours Sincerely
...
...could enclose a photo of the ... I Still go down to see ... almost every home Game
yours sincerely
CHRISTOPHER JARRETT

Dear Harry Carpenter
Thankyou for forwarding our letter to Dave Boy Green.
What is your favourite Bible passage, verse or story? Why did you chose that one?
We are putting all the answers in a book.
We've got replies from Prince charles, the pope, The two Ronnies and about 25 others so far.
Its fun getting letters
I hope you will join in.
Yours sincerely
Peter Coles (Age 12)

...I'm CRAZey over y... CRAZey over you I... And could you p... Thank you. yo...

Dear Una Stubbs,
I hope you are not too busy to answer this letter. In our school we have a writing group. I am one of them. Among other books we have written are: 'Home made prayers' and 'Love at a bus-stop.' We have also made a television programme called 'Funny People.'
Our teacher Janet Green has asked us to write to somebody who is famous. I chose you. What we want you to do is choose your favourite passage from the 'Bible'. It may be because of an incident that happened, or of something Funny that happened, to you.
We are thinking of calling it 'Best Bible Bits'. Send a letter stating which one you chose and why you chose it to us. You We hope you will join in, and if you do send a letter back we will be very thankful.
Yours faithfully,
Mark Lridge. (13)
P.S. could you also send a photo of your-self with the letter.
... of you and your ...
P.S.S. I have sent a photo of me. and you can keep it. I have enclosed a stamp so that you can reply.
This is the photo of me.

remembered, and that is why we have mainly used it in this book; it is the one that many people quoted in their replies. The project did encourage us, however, to look at other versions and see how they were different. You may want to do the same; to start you off, we have selected a modern translation, the **Good News Bible**, for some of our extracts.

When we began, the fear was that no one would reply or that everyone would choose the same verses. People did reply and I wish sincerely to thank them. They did choose different passages; though, obviously, there are some predictable favourites like the twenty-third psalm, we found that we had in fact collected readings from right though the Bible – Genesis to Revelation. (I was sad that nobody chose the 'Acts of the Apostles' because that's my favourite book. But nobody thought to write to me.)

I can't remember the exact moment when we decided we were making a book. In fact we were so caught up in it all that we nearly forgot to enter the competition which had started us off. We only just made the closing date.

The title has been **Best Bible Bits** since the beginning. Our boys always use the term 'my best' to mean 'my favourite'. I have complained about this butchering of the English language for years. I nagged them out of using the phrase in the letters but when the replies began to arrive, they always asked, 'Who's written?' and 'What's their best bit?' Somebody, seeing the working title **Best Bible Bits** on the folder, remarked 'Try saying that when you've had a few pints.' I had to concede that it was a memorable title. What clinched it in my mind, however, was when a boy in 1C asked, 'Miss, which bit of the Bible do you think is God's Best Bit?' Una Stubbs gave us a thought worth repeating. She chose 'The Song of Solomon' – a passage which she had laughed at while at school but which she had grown to appreciate in later years.

'I suppose,' said one lad, 'the Bible is like all books; it's always worth a second look. You never know. It might mean something different next time round.'

Janet Green

The Letter Writers . . .

Stephen Adams, Darren Anderson, Declan Ainger, Iain Aitchison, Gary Atwill, Shaun Banbury, Robert Barry, Salman Bhaidani, Richard Bowden, Mortimer Boyce, Peter Boyce, Jason Boylan, David Boyle, Anthony David Brown, Matthew Bryant, Steve Bryant, Karl Butler, Shaun Caradine, Fred Carpenter, Melvyn Coghlan, Peter Coles, Mark Cridge, Michael Cudden, Lee Doble, Gary Elstone, Lee Elstone, Simon Eckersley, Michael Farrell, Adrian Goodman, Lee Green, Richard Griffin, David Griffiths, Paul Griffiths, Malcolm Hannan, Mark Hannan, Darren Hawker, Martin Hawker, Ian Hayes, Martin Hill, Dorian Holbrook, Jason Holloway, Darren Hooper, Ivor Horton, Martin Lee Isles, Richard Jaap, Christopher Jarrett, Wayne Jarrett, Tak Wah Jim, Lee Johnson, Alistair Johnstone, Andrew Lear, Adrian Lewis, Richard Long 1C, Richard Long 4A, Lee Mallard, Neil Marsh, Clive Martin, Frank McClory, Jason Miles, Nigel Moore, Gary Morgan, Darren Morris 1A, Darren Morris 2C, Daniel Mullin, Robert Ogden, Anthony O'Reilly, Kevin O'Toole, Geoffrey Pearce, Simon Piper, Mark Potter, Lisette Price, Darren Reeves, Paul Sanki, Patrick Searle, Paul Slade, Christopher Smith, Dean Stenner, Robert Stenner, Simon Stevens, Andrew Thomas, Darren Thomas, Mark Thomas, Nigel Thomas, Emil Toth, Ricky Trotham, Jason Wall, Andrew Wallace, Anthony Wilkes, Lee Williams, Mark Wood.

The Old Testament

Kenny Everett

BBC

BRITISH BROADCASTING CORPORATION
ARIEL HOUSE 74A CHARLOTTE STREET LONDON W1
TELEPHONE 01-580 4468 TELEX: 265781
TELEGRAMS AND CABLES: BROADCASTS LONDON TELEX
POSTAL ADDRESS BBC LONDON W1A 1AA

Dear Jason,

Thank you for your letter to Kenny Everett. He has asked me to reply.

Kenny says that his favourite part of the Bible is Genesis. He thinks that God is very clever to have made everything in six days.

I have enclosed a photo of Kenny and I hope you like it.

Yours sincerely,

Rosalind Allen

(Rosalind Allen)
PRODUCTION SECRETARY

Jason Miles,
Greenway Boys' School,
Doncaster Road,
Westbury-on-Trym,
Bristol,
BS10 5PY

In the beginning God created the heaven and the earth.

And the earth was without form, and void; and darkness was upon the face of the deep. And the Spirit of God moved upon the face of the waters.

And God said, Let there be light: and there was light.

And God saw the light, that it was good: and God divided the light from the darkness.

And God called the light Day, and the darkness he called Night. And the evening and the morning were the first day.

And God said, Let there be a firmament in the midst of the waters, and let it divide the waters from the waters.

And God made the firmament and divided the waters which were under the firmament from the waters which were above the firmament: and it was so.

And God called the firmament Heaven. And the evening and the morning were the second day.

And God said, Let the waters under the heaven be gathered together unto one place, and let the dry land appear: and it was so.

And God called the dry land Earth; and the gathering together of the waters called he Seas: and God saw that it was good.

And God said, Let the earth bring forth grass, the herb yielding seed, and the fruit tree yielding fruit after his kind, whose seed is in itself, upon the earth: and it was so.

And the earth brought forth grass, and herb yielding seed after his kind, and the tree yielding fruit whose seed was in itself, after his kind: And God saw that it was good.

And the evening and the morning were the third day.

And God said, Let there be lights in the firmament of the heaven to divide the day from the night; and let them be signs, and for seasons, and for days, and years:

And let them be for lights in the firmament of the heaven to give light upon the earth: and it was so.

And God made two great lights; the greater light to rule the day, and the lesser light to rule the night: he made the stars also.

And God set them in the firmament of the heaven to give light upon the earth.

And to rule over the day and over the night, and to divide the light from the darkness: and God saw that it was good.

And the evening and the morning were the fourth day.

And God said, Let the waters bring forth abundantly the moving creature that hath life and fowl that may fly above the earth in the open firmament of heaven.

And God created great whales, and every living creature that moveth, which the waters brought forth abundantly, after their kind, and every winged fowl after his kind: and God saw that it was good.

And God blessed them, saying, Be fruitful, and multiply, and fill the waters in the seas, and let fowl multiply in the earth.

And the evening and the morning were the fifth day.

And God said, Let the earth bring forth the living creature after his kind, cattle and creeping thing, and beast of the earth after his kind: and it was so.

And God made the beast of the earth after his kind, and cattle after their kind, and every thing that creepeth upon the earth after his kind: and God saw that it was good.

And God said, Let us make man in our image, after our likeness: and let them have dominion over the fish of the sea, and over the fowl of the air, and over the cattle, and over all the earth, and over every creeping thing that creepeth upon the earth.

So God created man in his own image, in the image of God created he him; male and female created he them.

And God blessed them, and God said unto them, Be fruitful, and multiply, and replenish the earth, and subdue it: and have dominion over the fish of the sea, and over the fowl of the air, and over every living thing that moveth upon the earth.

And God said, Behold, I have given you every herb bearing seed, which is upon the face of all the earth, and every tree, in which is the fruit of a tree yielding seed; to you it shall be for meat.

And to every beast of the earth, and to every fowl of the air, and to every thing that creepeth upon the earth, wherein there is life, I have given every green herb for meat: and it was so.

And God saw every thing that he had made, and, behold, it was very good. And the evening and the morning were the sixth day.

(Genesis 1)

Desmond Morris

THIS IS MY FAVOURITE PASSAGE FROM THE BIBLE:
THE STORY OF THE GARDEN OF EDEN....BECAUSE IT IS
SO MYSTERIOUS! GENESIS, 2. +3.

8 ¶ And the LORD God planted a garden eastward in Eden; and there he put the man whom he had formed.

9 And out of the ground made the LORD God to grow every tree that is pleasant to the sight, and good for food; the tree of life also in the midst of the garden, and the tree of knowledge of good and evil.

10 And a river went out of Eden to water the garden;

15 And the LORD God took the man, and put him into the garden of Eden to dress it and to keep it.

16 And the LORD God commanded the man, saying, Of every tree of the garden thou mayest freely eat:

17 But of the tree of the knowledge of good and evil, thou shalt not eat of it: for in the day that thou eatest thereof thou shalt surely die.

Why not?

18 ¶ And the LORD God said, *It is* not good that the man should be alone; I will make him an help meet for him.

19 And out of the ground the LORD God formed every beast of the field, and every fowl of the air; and brought *them* unto Adam to see what he would call them: and whatsoever Adam called every living creature, that *was* the name thereof.

20 And Adam gave names to all cattle, and to the fowl of the air, and to every beast of the field; but for Adam there was not found an help meet for him.

21 And the LORD God caused a deep sleep to fall upon Adam, and he slept: and he took one of his ribs, and closed up the flesh instead thereof;

Why a rib?

22 And the rib, which the LORD God had taken from man, made he a woman, and brought her unto the man.

23 And Adam said, This *is* now bone of my bones, and flesh of my flesh: she shall be called Woman, because she was taken out of Man.

24 Therefore shall a man leave his father and his mother, and shall cleave unto his wife: and they shall be one flesh.

25 And they were both naked, the man and his wife, and were not ashamed.

CHAPTER 3.

1 The serpent deceiveth Eve. 6 Man's shameful fall. 9 God arraigneth them. 14 The serpent is cursed. 15 The promised seed. 16 The punishment of mankind. 21 Their first clothing. 22 Their casting out of paradise.

NOW the serpent was more subtil than any beast of the field which the LORD God had made. And he said unto the woman, Yea, hath God said, Ye shall not eat of every tree of the garden?

Why a snake?

2 And the woman said unto the serpent, We may eat of the fruit of the trees of the garden:

3 But of the fruit of the tree which *is* in the midst of the garden, God hath said, Ye shall not eat of it, neither shall ye touch it, lest ye die.

4 And the serpent said unto the woman, Ye shall not surely die:

5 For God doth know that in the day ye eat thereof, then your eyes shall be opened, and ye shall be as gods, knowing good and evil.

6 And when the woman saw that the tree *was* good for food, and that it *was* pleasant to the eyes, and a tree to be desired to make *one* wise, she took of the fruit thereof, and did eat, and gave also unto her husband with her; and he did eat.

Why her? & not him?

7 And the eyes of them both were opened, and they knew that they *were* naked; and they sewed fig leaves together, and made themselves aprons.

Why?

8 And they heard the voice of the LORD God walking in the garden in the cool of the day: and Adam and his wife hid themselves from the presence of the LORD God amongst the trees of the garden.

9 And the LORD God called unto Adam, and said unto him, Where *art* thou?

10 And he said, I heard thy voice in the garden, and I was afraid, because I *was* naked; and I hid myself.

Why?

11 And he said, Who told thee that thou *wast* naked? Hast thou eaten of the tree, whereof I commanded thee that thou shouldest not eat?

12 And the man said, The woman whom thou gavest *to be* with me, she gave me of the tree, and I did eat.

13 And the LORD God said unto the woman, What *is* this *that* thou hast done? And the woman said, The serpent beguiled me, and I did eat.

14 And the LORD God said unto the serpent, Because thou hast done this, thou *art* cursed above all cattle, and above every beast of the field; upon thy belly shalt thou go, and dust shalt thou eat all the days of thy life:

15 And I will put enmity between thee and the woman, and between thy seed and her seed; it shall bruise thy head, and thou shalt bruise his heel.

Why?

16 Unto the woman he said, I will greatly multiply thy sorrow and thy conception; in sorrow thou shalt bring forth children; and thy desire *shall be* to thy husband, and he shall rule over thee.

17 And unto Adam he said, Because thou hast hearkened unto the voice of thy wife, and hast eaten of the tree, of which I commanded thee, saying, Thou shalt not eat of it: cursed *is* the ground for thy sake; in sorrow shalt thou eat *of* it all the days of thy life;

Why such cruelty?

18 Thorns also and thistles shall it bring forth to thee; and thou shalt eat the herb of the field;

19 In the sweat of thy face shalt thou eat bread, till thou return unto the ground; for out of it wast thou taken: for dust thou *art*, and unto dust shalt thou return.

20 And Adam called his wife's name Eve; because she was the mother of all living.

21 Unto Adam also and to his wife did the LORD God make coats of skins, and clothed them.

22 ¶ And the LORD God said, Behold, the man is become as one of us, to know good and evil: and now, lest he put forth his hand, and take also of the tree of life, and eat, and live for ever:

23 Therefore the LORD God sent him forth from the garden of Eden, to till the ground from whence he was taken.

24 So he drove out the man; and he placed at the east of the garden of Eden Cherubims, and a flaming sword which turned every way, to keep the way of the tree of life.

BEST WISHES FROM DESMOND MORRIS.....

Desmond Morris

Sandor Elès

Central Independent Television plc
Central House
Broad Street
Birmingham B1 2JP

CENTRAL

Telephone 021-643 9898
Telex 338966
Cables and telegrams:
Television Birmingham

Dear Lee Elstone,

The two most important statements in the Bible are as follows.

I { (1) "I AM THAT I AM".
(1A) "MY FATHER & I ARE ONE."

II { (2) "THE KINGDOM OF HEAVEN IS WITHIN"

These I've found immensely useful throughout my life & meditation upon these can lead to enlightenment; — which is the goal.

Thanks for your letter.

Sandor Elès

And Moses said unto God, Behold, when I come unto the children of Israel, and shall say unto them, The God of your fathers hath sent me unto you; and they shall say to me, What is his name? what shall I say unto them?

And God said to Moses I AM THAT I AM: and he said, Thus shalt thou say unto the children of Israel, I AM hath sent me to you.

(Exodus 3.14, 15)

Ernie Wise

Dear Colin

My favourite BIBLE passage is the "Ten Commandments" read it and live by it you will not get better advice.

Good luck

Ernie

God spoke, and these were his words: "I am the Lord your God who brought you out of Egypt, where you were slaves.

"Worship no god but me.

"Do not make for yourselves images of anything in heaven or on earth or in the water under the earth. Do not bow down to any idol or worship it, because I am the Lord your God and I tolerate no rivals. I bring punishment on those who hate me and on their descendants down to the third and fourth generation. But I show my love to thousands of generations of those who love me and obey my laws.

"Do not use my name for evil purposes, for I, the Lord your God, will punish anyone who misuses my name.

"Observe the Sabbath and keep it holy. You have six days in which to do your work, but the seventh day is a day of rest dedicated to me. On that day no-one is to work – neither you, your children, your slaves, your animals, nor the foreigners who live in your country. In six days I, the Lord, made the earth, the sky, the sea, and everything in them, but on the seventh day I rested. That is why I, the Lord, blessed the Sabbath and made it holy.

"Respect your father and your mother, so that you may live a long time in the land that I am giving you.

"Do not commit murder.

"Do not commit adultery.

"Do not steal.

"Do not accuse anyone falsely.

"Do not desire another man's house; do not desire his wife, his slaves, his cattle, his donkeys, or anything else that he owns."

(Exodus 20, 1 – 17. Good News Bible)

Jill Gascoine

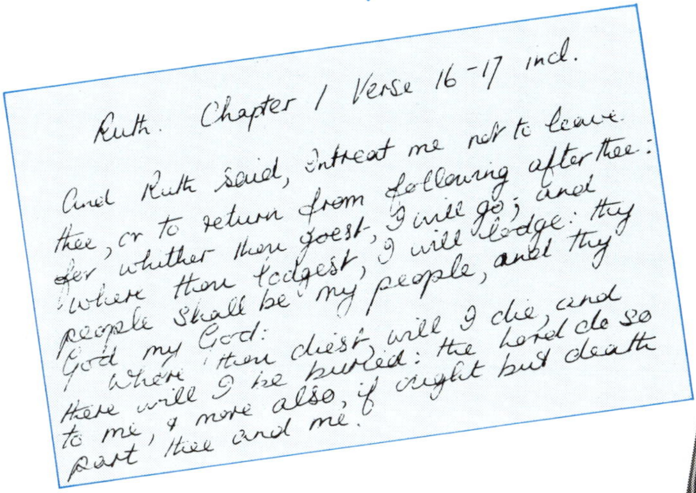
Ruth. Chapter 1 Verse 16-17 incl.

And Ruth said, Intreat me not to leave thee, or to return from following after thee: for whither thou goest, I will go; and where thou lodgest, I will lodge: thy people shall be my people, and thy God my God:
Where thou diest will I die, and there will I be buried: the Lord do so to me, & more also, if ought but death part thee and me.

(Naomi, an Israelite widow, has been living in the land of Moab, and her two sons, now dead, had married Moabite girls. Now Naomi is setting out to return to Israel.)

And Naomi said unto her two daughters in law, Go, return each to her mother's house: the Lord deal kindly with you, as ye have dealt with the dead, and with me.

The Lord grant you that ye may find rest, each of you in the house of her husband. Then she kissed them; and they lifted up their voice, and wept.

And they said unto her, Surely we will return with thee unto thy people.

And Naomi said, Turn again, my daughters: why will ye go with me? are there yet any more sons in my womb, that they may be your husbands?

Turn again, my daughters, go your way; for I am too old to have an husband.

If I should say, I have hope, if I should have an husband also to night, and should also bear sons;

Would ye tarry for them till they were grown? would ye stay for them from having husbands? nay, my daughters; for it grieveth me much for your sakes that the hand of the Lord is gone out against me.

And they lifted up their voice, and wept again: and Orpah kissed her mother in law; but Ruth clave unto her.

And she said, Behold thy sister in law is gone back unto her people, and unto her gods: return thou after thy sister in law.

And Ruth said, Intreat me not to leave thee, or to return from following after thee: for whither thou goest, I will go; and where thou lodgest, I will lodge: thy people shall be my people, and thy God my God: Where thou diest, I will die, and there will I be buried: the Lord do so to me, and more also, if ought but death part thee and me.

(Ruth 1, 8 – 17)

The Chief Rabbi

ב"ה

OFFICE OF THE CHIEF RABBI

TELEPHONE:
01-387 1066 (4 LINES)
CABLES:
CHIRABINAT LONDON WC1

ADLER HOUSE,
TAVISTOCK SQUARE,
LONDON, WC1H 9HN

Martin Hill
Greenway Boys' Comprehensive School
Doncaster Road
Westbury on Trym
Bristol BS10 5PY

Dear Martin

The story I find most fascinating in the Hebrew Bible is the famous Judgement of Solomon. You will find it in the third chapter of the First Book of Kings.

I wish you every success in your venture, and I hope it will encourage people to read the Bible and to live by its precepts.

Yours sincerely

Sir Immanuel Jakobovits
Chief Rabbi

Then came two women, that were harlots, unto the king, and stood before him. And the one woman said, O my lord, I and this woman dwell in one house; and I was delivered of a child with her in the house.

And it came to pass the third day after that I was delivered, that this woman was delivered also: and we were together; there was no stranger with us in the house, save we two in the house.

And this woman's child died in the night; because she overlaid it. And she arose at midnight, and took my son from beside me, while thine handmaid slept, and laid it in her bosom, and laid her dead child in my bosom. And when I rose in the morning to give my child suck, behold, it was dead: but when I had considered it in the morning, behold, it was not my son, which I did bear.

And the other woman said, Nay; but the living is my son, and the dead is thy son. And this said, No; but the dead is thy son, and the living is my son. Thus they spake before the king . . .

And the king said, Bring me a sword. And they brought a sword before the king. And the king said, Divide the living child in two, and give half to the one, and half to the other.

Then spake the woman whose the living child was unto the king, for her bowels yearned upon her son, and she said, O my lord, give her the living child, and in no wise slay it. But the other said, Let it be neither mine nor thine, but divide it.

Then the king answered and said, Give her the living child, and in no wise slay it: she is the mother thereof.

And all Israel heard of the judgment which the king had judged; and they feared the king: for they saw that the wisdom of God was in him, to do judgment.

(I Kings 3. 16 – 22, 24 – 28.)

(Esther, a Jewish girl, daughter of the wise Mordecai, is married to the powerful Persian king Xerxes. His wicked prime minister, Haman, has plotted to have Mordecai and all the Jews in the kingdom killed. Esther takes her life in her hands to plead with the king, and invites him, together with Haman, to a banquet.)

Over the wine the king asked her again, "Now, Queen Esther, what do you want? Tell me and you shall have it. I'll even give you half the empire." Queen Esther answered, "If it please Your Majesty to grant my humble request, my wish is that I may live and my people may live. My people and I have been sold for slaughter. If it were nothing more serious than being sold into slavery, I would have kept quiet and not bothered you about it; but we are about to be destroyed – exterminated."

Then King Xerxes asked Queen Esther, "Who dares to do such a thing? Where is this man?"

Esther answered, "Our enemy, our persecutor, is this evil man Haman!" Haman stared at the king and queen in terror. The king got up in a fury, left the room, and went outside to the palace gardens. Haman could see that the king was determined to punish him for this, so he stayed behind to beg Queen Esther for his life. He had just thrown himself down on Esther's couch to beg for mercy, when the king came back into the room from the gardens. Seeing this, the king cried out, "Is this man going to rape the queen right here in front of me, in my own palace?"

The king had no sooner said this that the eunuchs covered Haman's head. Then one of them, who was named Harbonah, said, "Haman even went so far as to build a gallows at his house so that he could hang Mordecai, who saved Your Majesty's life. And it's twenty-two metres tall!"

"Hang Haman on it!" the king commanded.

So Haman was hanged on the gallows that he had built for Mordecai.

(Esther 7. 2 – 10. Good News Bible)

Esther Rantzen

BBC tv

BRITISH BROADCASTING CORPORATION
LIME GROVE STUDIOS LONDON W12 7RJ
TELEPHONE 01-743 8000 TELEX: 265781
TELEGRAMS AND CABLES: TELECASTS LONDON TELEX

2nd November 1983

Mr. B. Stenner,
Greenway Boys' Comprehensive School,
Doncaster Road,
Westbury-on-Trym,
Bristol.
BS10 5PY

Dear Bobby,

My favourite part of the Bible is the Book of Esther - it is a marvellous story, like Cinderella, of an ordinary girl who becomes a princess - it is the first recorded beauty contest, which was won with her intelligence - and obviously I have had to read it quite often myself as I was named after her!

Best wishes.

Yours sincerely,

Esther Rantzen

(Esther Rantzen)

Wendy Craig

The Lord is my shepherd; I shall not want.

He maketh me to lie down in green pastures: he leadeth me beside the still waters.

He restoreth my soul: he leadeth me in the paths of righteousness for his name's sake.

Yea, though I walk through the valley of the shadow of death, I will fear no evil: for thou art with me; thy rod and thy staff they comfort me.

Thou preparest a table before me in the presence of mine enemies: thou anointest my head with oil; my cup runneth over.

Surely goodness and mercy shall follow me all the days of my life: and I will dwell in the house of the Lord for ever.

(Psalm 23)

BBC Television Centre
Wood Lane
London W.12.

Dear Richard Lovell,

Thank you for writing to me. My favourite reading from the Bible is Psalm twenty three.

In the sort of work I do I often have moments when I'm very nervous and apprehensive – for instance before making my entrance on a first night. I repeat the Psalm to myself quietly in the dressing room and I'm quite sure I'm given strength to aproach my work with a positive attitude, knowing that God is with me to help and support me.

Best wishes to you, the other children, and the teachers at your school.

Yours sincerely,

Wendy Craig.

Barry Sheene

CSS Promotions Limited

1 Bedford Street,
London WC2E 9HD
Telephone 01-379 7989
Telex 22432 (CSS PRO G)

LMP/FG

Mr N Marsh
Greenway Boys' Comprehensive School
Doncaster Road
Westbury-on-Trym
Bristol
BS10 5PY

Dear Neil

Thank you for your letter addressed to Barry Sheene, which has been passed to me for reply.

I have spoken to Barry about your letter, and his immediate reply was that he particularly remembers Psalm 23. He is not sure why it should be significant to him though he feels that because it is a short but clear psalm, it has stuck in his mind.

Do hope you can use this in your book, and that the publication will be successful. As requested, herewith a photo of Barry which he has autographed for you.

Yours sincerely

Linda Patterson

Directors:
Barrie Gill BA (Chairman & Chief Executive) Andrew Marriott John M Mills Michael Tee
Graham Bridgwater BA

Terry Scott

Terry Scott

Dear Chris,

Terry has asked me to reply to your letter and to tell you that his favourite Bible Passage is the 23 Psalm. "The Lord is my Shepherd".

Read it, slowly line by line and you will realise why that is his choice.

Please convey Terry's best wishes to your teacher Miss Green.

Yours truly

pp Terry Scott.

Geoff Hughes

ehensive School,
...-Trym,
...istol BS10 5PY.

Dear Robert,

Thanks for your letter. My favourite is the 23rd Psalm because it is a great comfort when life gets difficult and there are problems.

To get everybody's autographs on Coronation Street, write to Leita Donn, Press Office, Granada T.V., Manchester, and she will help you.

I have enclosed a photograph. Hope you like it.

Yours sincerely,

Geoff

The Rt. Hon. Margaret Thatcher

10 DOWNING STREET

Dear Mr. Hall,

I am writing on the Prime Minister's behalf to thank you for your recent letter requesting information about her favourite Bible passage.

I have pleasure in sending you two verses from Psalm 46 which she particularly likes, and a photograph.

With best wishes,

Yours sincerely

Derek Howe

Derek Howe
Political Office

Martin Hall Esq

God is our refuge and strength, a very present help in trouble.

Therefore will not we fear, though the earth be removed, and though the mountains be carried into the midst of the sea;

Though the waters thereof roar and be troubled, though the mountains shake with the swelling thereof.

There is a river, the streams whereof shall make glad the city of God, the holy place of the tabernacles of the most High.

God is in the midst of her; she shall not be moved: God shall help, and that right early.

The heathen raged, the kingdoms were moved: he uttered his voice, the earth melted.

The Lord of hosts is with us; the God of Jacob is our refuge.

Come, behold the works of the Lord, what desolations he hath made in the earth.

He maketh wars to cease unto the end of the earth; he breaketh the bow, and cutteth the spear in sunder; he burneth the chariot of fire.

Be still, and know that I am God; I will be exalted among the heathen, I will be exalted in the earth.

The Lord of hosts is with us; the God of Jacob is our refuge.

(Psalm 46)

Sue Lloyd

Central Independent Television plc
Central House
Broad Street
Birmingham B1 2JP

CENTRAL

Our Ref: SL/SR

Dee Elstone Esq.,
c/o P.B. Godfrey Esq.,
Headmaster,
Avon Education Service,
Queensway Boys' Comprehensive School,
Doncaster Road,
Westbury-on-Tryme,
Bristol. BS10 5PY.

Dear Dee,

Thank you for your letter.

My favourite passage from The Bible is from Ecclesiastes Chapter 3.

To every thing there is a season, and a time to
every purpose under the heaven:
A time to be born, and a time to die; a time
to plant, and a time to pluck up that which
is planted;
A time to kill, and a time to heal; a time to
break down, and a time to build up;
A time to weep, and a time to laugh; a time
to mourn, and a time to dance;
A time to cast away stones, and a time to
gather stones together, a time to embrace,
and a time to refrain from embracing;
A time to get, and a time to lose, a time to keep,
and a time to cast away;
A time to love, and a time to sew; a time to
keep silence, and a time to speak;
A time of love, and a time to hate; a time of war,
and a time of peace.

I have chosen this passage because it was the first excerpt from The Bible that I was taught, and it brings back happy memories of my parents.

I was sorry to hear that your school will have to close down and I would like to wish you good luck with your book.

Yours sincerely,

Sue Lloyd

Sue Lloyd

Neil Kinnock

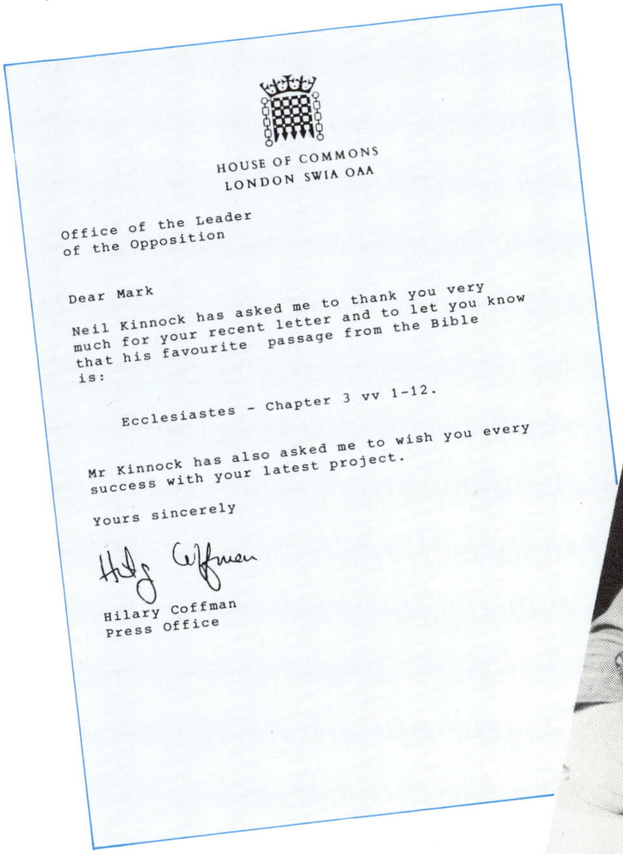
HOUSE OF COMMONS
LONDON SW1A 0AA

Office of the Leader
of the Opposition

Dear Mark

Neil Kinnock has asked me to thank you very much for your recent letter and to let you know that his favourite passage from the Bible is:

Ecclesiastes - Chapter 3 vv 1-12.

Mr Kinnock has also asked me to wish you every success with your latest project.

Yours sincerely

Hilary Coffman

Hilary Coffman
Press Office

To every thing there is a season, and a time to every purpose under the heaven: A time to be born and a time to die; a time to plant, and a time to pluck up that which is planted;

A time to kill, and a time to heal; a time to break down, and a time to build up;

A time to weep, and a time to laugh; a time to mourn, and a time to dance;

A time to cast away stones, and a time to gather stones together; a time to embrace, and a time to refrain from embracing;

A time to get, and a time to lose; a time to keep, and a time to cast away;

A time to rend, and a time to sew; a time to keep silence, and a time to speak;

A time to love and a time to hate; a time of war, and a time of peace.

What profit hath he that worketh in that wherein he laboureth?

I have seen the travail, which God hath given to the sons of men to be exercised in it.

He hath made every thing beautiful in his time: also he hath set the world in their heart, so that no man can find out the work that God maketh from the beginning to the end.

I know that there is no good in them, but for a man to rejoice, and to do good in his life.

(Ecclesiastes 3. 1 – 12)

Una Stubbs

Behold, thou art fair, my love; behold, thou art fair; thou hast doves' eyes within thy locks: thy hair is as a flock of goats, that appear from mount Gilead.

Thy teeth are like a flock of sheep that are even shorn, which came up from the washing; whereof every one bear twins, and none is barren among them.

(Song of Solomon, 4. 1 – 2)

Dear Mark

Thankyou for your letter.

I love the "Songs of Solomon" especially verse 4 where he describes his love as having teeth as white as newly shorn sheeps wool with out one missing!! I remember when I was young thinking that very funny but I find it rather a beautiful description now!

Thankyou for choosing me to write to.

love

Una x

Jimmy Savile

The people that walked in darkness have seen a great light: they that dwell in the land of the shadow of death, upon them hath the light shined . . .

For unto us a child is born, unto us a son is given: and the government shall be upon his shoulder: and his name shall be called Wonderful, Counsellor, The mighty God, The everlasting Father, The Prince of Peace.

Of the increase of his government and peace there shall be no end, upon the throne of David, and upon his kingdom, to order it, and to establish it with judgment and with justice from henceforth even for ever. The zeal of the Lord of hosts will perform this.

(Isaiah 9. 2, 6, 7)

Leeds Western Health Authority

The General Infirmary at Leeds
Great George Street, Leeds LS1 3EX
Telephone 0532-432799

Mr Martin Hill
Greenway Boys Comprehensive School
Doncaster Road
Westbury-on-Trym
BRISTOL

Enquiries to:
Extension:
Our ref:
Your ref:
Date:

Dear Martin

Many thanks for your letter.

One of my favourite passages is Isaiah, Chapter 9, verses 2, 6 and 7.

Sincerely

Jimmy Savile

Gordon Jackson

Ho, everyone that thirsteth, come ye to the waters, and he that hath no money; come ye, buy and eat; yea, come buy wine and milk without money and without price.

Wherefore do ye spend money for that which is not bread? and your labour for that which satisfieth not? hearken diligently unto me, and eat ye that which is good, and let your soul delight itself in fatness.

Incline your ear, and come unto me: hear, and your soul shall live; and I will make an everlasting covenant with you, even the sure mercies of David. Behold, I have given him for a witness to the people, a leader and commander to the people.

Behold, thou shalt call a nation that thou knowest not, and nations that knew not thee shall run unto thee because of the Lord thy God, and for the Holy One of Israel; for he hath glorified thee.

Seek ye the Lord while he may be found, call ye upon him while he is near: Let the wicked forsake his way, and the unrighteous man his thoughts: and let him return unto the Lord, and he will have mercy upon him; and to our God, for he will abundantly pardon.

For my thoughts are not your thoughts, neither are your ways my ways, saith the Lord.

For as the heavens are higher than the earth, so are my ways higher than your ways, and my thoughts than your thoughts.

For as the rain cometh down, and the snow from heaven, and returneth not thither, but watereth the earth, and maketh it bring forth and bud, that it may give seed to the sower, and bread to the eater;

GORDON JACKSON

Dear Tony, Thank you for your letter.

One of my favourite passages in The Bible is "Ho, Every one that thirsteth, Come ye to the waters!" (Isaiah – Chapter 55).

I vividly remember, as a wee boy, having to read this chapter from the pulpit at a Children's Service at my local church (North Kelvinside) in Glasgow. Although I was very nervous, I enjoyed the experience enormously! Which only goes to prove, that I was a ham actor, even at the ripe age of ten!

Every success with your book!

Yours sincerely,

Gordon Jackson

So shall my word be that goeth forth out of my mouth: it shall not return to me void, but it shall accomplish that which I please, and it shall prosper in the thing whereto I sent it.

For ye shall go out with joy, and be led forth with peace: the mountains and the hills shall break forth before you into singing, and all the trees of the field shall clap their hands.

Instead of the thorn shall come up the fir tree, and instead of the brier shall come up the myrtle tree: and it shall be to the Lord for a name, for an everlasting sign that shall not be cut off.

(Isaiah 55)

Bob Monkhouse

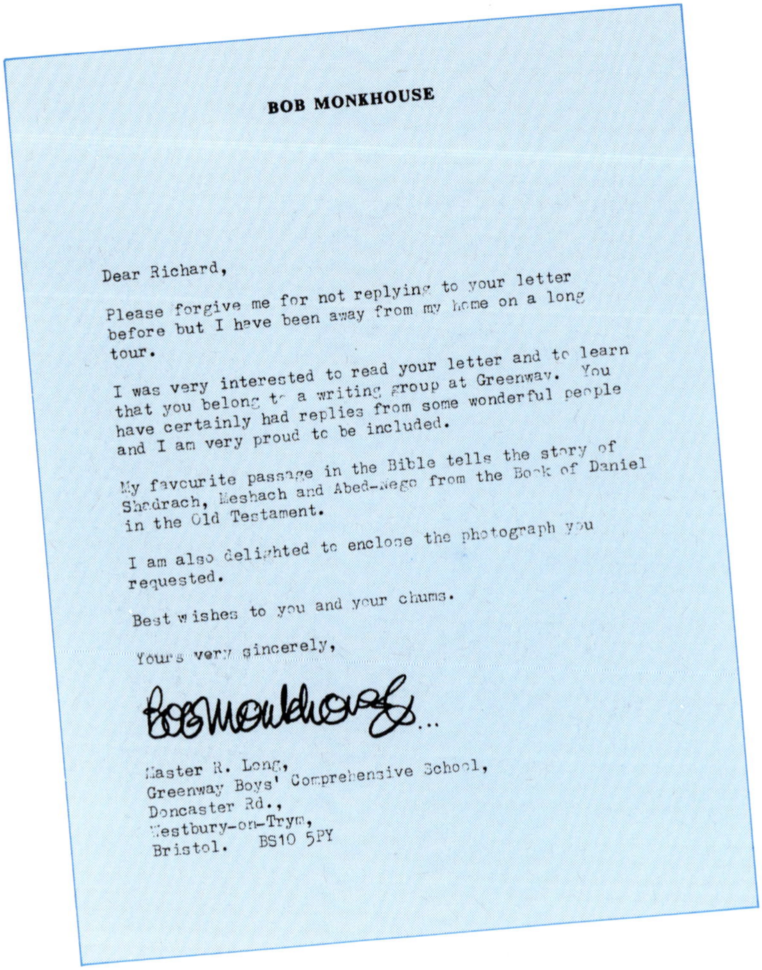

BOB MONKHOUSE

Dear Richard,

Please forgive me for not replying to your letter before but I have been away from my home on a long tour.

I was very interested to read your letter and to learn that you belong to a writing group at Greenway. You have certainly had replies from some wonderful people and I am very proud to be included.

My favourite passage in the Bible tells the story of Shadrach, Meshach and Abed-Nego from the Book of Daniel in the Old Testament.

I am also delighted to enclose the photograph you requested.

Best wishes to you and your chums.

Yours very sincerely,

Bob Monkhouse...

Master R. Long,
Greenway Boys' Comprehensive School,
Doncaster Rd.,
Westbury-on-Trym,
Bristol. BS10 5PY

King Nebuchadnezzar had a gold statue made, twenty-seven metres high and nearly three metres wide, and he had it set up in the plain of Dura in the province of Babylon. Then the king gave orders for all his officials to come together – the princes, governors, lieutenant-governors, commissioners, treasurers, judges, magistrates, and all the other officials of the provinces. They were to attend the dedication of the statue which King Nebuchadnezzar had set up. When all these officials gathered for the dedication and stood in front of the statue, a herald announced in a loud voice, "People of all nations, races and languages! You will hear the sound of trumpets, followed by the playing of oboes, lyres, zithers, and harps; and then all the other instruments will join in. As soon as the music starts, you are to bow down and worship the gold statue that King Nebuchadnezzar has set up. Anyone who does not bow down and worship will immediately be thrown into a blazing furnace." And so, as soon as they heard the sound of the instruments, the people of all the nations, races and languages bowed down and worshipped the gold statue which King Nebuchadnezzar had set up.

It was then that some Babylonians took the opportunity to denounce the Jews. They said to King Nebuchadnezzar, "May Your Majesty live for ever! Your Majesty has issued an order that as soon as the music starts, everyone is to bow down and worship the gold statue, and that anyone who does not bow down and worship it is to be thrown into a blazing furnace. There are some Jews whom you put in charge of the province of Babylon – Shadrach, Meshach, and Abednego – who are disobeying Your Majesty's orders. They do not worship your god or bow down to the statue you set up."

At that, the king flew into a rage and ordered the three men to be brought before him. He said to them, "Shadrach, Meshach, and Abednego, is it true that you refuse to worship my god and to bow down to the gold statue I have set up? Now then, as soon as you hear the sound of the trumpets, oboes, lyres, zithers, harps, and all the other instruments, bow down and worship the statue. If you do not, you will immediately be thrown into a blazing furnace. Do you think there is any god who can save you?"

Shadrach, Meshach, and Abednego answered, "Your Majesty, we will not try to defend ourselves. If the God whom we serve is able to save us from the blazing furnace and from your power, then he will. But even if he doesn't, Your Majesty may be sure that we will not worship your god, and we will not bow down to the gold statue that you have set up."

Then Nebuchadnezzar lost his temper, and his face turned red with anger at Shadrach, Meshach, and Abednego. So he ordered his men to heat the furnace seven times hotter than usual. And he commanded the strongest men in his army to tie the three men up and throw them into the blazing furnace. So they tied them up, fully dressed – shirts, robes, caps, and all – and threw them into the blazing furnace. Now because the king had given strict orders for the furnace to be made extremely hot, the flames burnt up the guards who took the men to the furnace. Then Shadrach, Meshach, and Abednego, still tied up, fell into the heart of the blazing fire.

Suddenly Nebuchadnezzar leapt to his feet in amazement. He asked his officials, "Didn't we tie up three men and throw them into the blazing furnace?" They answered, "Yes, we did, Your Majesty."

"Then why do I see four men walking about in the fire?" he asked. "They are not tied up, and they show no signs of being hurt – and the fourth one looks like an angel."

So Nebuchadnezzar went up to the door of the blazing furnace and called out, "Shadrach! Meshach! Abednego! Servants of the Supreme God! Come out!" And they came out at once. All the princes, governors, lieutenant-governors, and other officials of the king gathered to look at the three men, who had not been harmed by the fire. Their hair was not singed, their clothes were not burnt, and there was no smell of smoke on them.

The king said, "Praise the God of Shadrach, Meshach, and Abednego! He sent his angel and rescued these men who serve and trust him. They disobeyed my orders and risked their lives rather than bow down and worship any god except their own.

"And now I command that if anyone of any nation, race, or language speaks disrespectfully of the God of Shadrach, Meshach, and Abednego, he is to be torn limb from limb, and his house is to be made a pile of ruins. There is no other god who can rescue like this."

And the king promoted Shadrach, Meshach, and Abednego to higher positions in the province of Babylon.

(Daniel 3. Good News Bible)

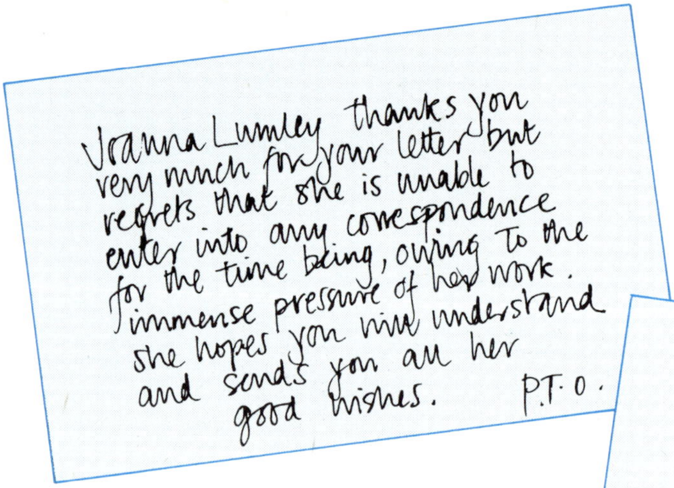
Joanna Lumley thanks you very much for your letter but regrets that she is unable to enter into any correspondence for the time being, owing to the immense pressure of her work. She hopes you will understand and sends you all her good wishes. P.T.O.

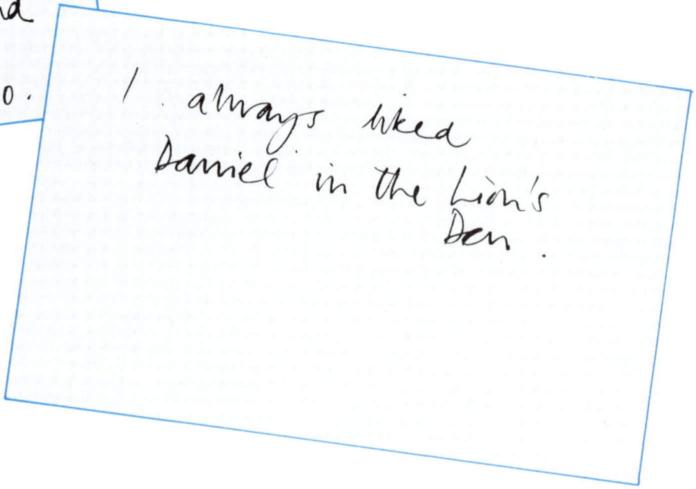
I always liked Daniel in the Lion's Den.

It pleased Darius to set over the kingdom a hundred and twenty princes, which should be over the whole kingdom;

And over these three presidents; of whom Daniel was first: that the princes might give accounts to them, and the king should have no damage.

Then this Daniel was preferred above the presidents and princes, because an excellent spirit was in him; and the king thought to set him over the whole realm.

Then the presidents and princes sought to find occasion against Daniel concerning the kingdom; but they could find none occasion nor fault; forasmuch as he was faithful, neither was there any error or fault in him.

Then said these men, We shall not find any occasion against this Daniel, except we find it against him concerning the law of his God.

Then these presidents and princes assembled together to the king, and said thus unto him, King Darius, live for ever.

All the presidents of the kingdom, the governors, and the princes, the counsellors, and the captains, have consulted together to establish a royal statute, and to make a firm decree, that whosoever shall ask a petition of any God or man for thirty days, save of thee, O king, he shall be cast into the den of lions.

Now, O king, establish the decree, and sign the writing, that it be not changed, according to the law of the Medes and Persians, which altereth not.

Wherefore King Darius signed the writing and the decree.

Now when Daniel knew that the writing was signed, he went into his house; and his windows being open in his chamber towards Jerusalem, he kneeled upon his knees three times a day, and prayed, and gave thanks before his God, as he did aforetime.

Then these men assembled, and found Daniel praying and making supplication before his God.

Then they came near, and spake before the king concerning the king's

Joanna Lumley

decree; Has thou not signed a decree, that every man that shall ask a petition of any God or man within thirty days, save of thee, O king, shall be cast into the den of lions? The king answered and said, The thing is true, according to the law of the Medes and Persians, which altereth not.

Then answered they and said before the king, That Daniel, which is of the children of the captivity of Judah, regardeth not thee, O king, nor the decree that thou hast signed, but maketh his petition three times a day.

Then the king, when he heard these words, was sore displeased with himself, and set his heart on Daniel to deliver him: and he laboured till the going down of the sun to deliver him.

Then these men assembled unto the king, and said unto the king, Know, O king, that the law of the Medes and Persians is, That no decree nor statute which the king establisheth may be changed.

Then the king commanded, and they brought Daniel, and cast him into the den of lions. Now the king spake and said unto Daniel, Thy God whom thou servest continually, he will deliver thee.

And a stone was brought, and laid upon the mouth of the den; and the king sealed it with his own signet, and with the signet of his lords; that the purpose might not be changed concerning Daniel.

Then the king went to his palace, and passed the night fasting: neither were instruments of musick brought before him: and his sleep went from him.

Then the king arose very early in the morning, and went in haste unto the den of lions.

And when he came to the den, he cried with a lamentable voice unto Daniel: and the king spake and said to Daniel, O Daniel, servant of the living God, is thy God, whom thou servest continually, able to deliver thee from the lions?

Then said Daniel unto the king, O king, live for ever.

My God hath sent his angel, and hath shut the lions' mouths, that they have not hurt me: forasmuch as before him innocency was found in me; and also before thee, O king, have I done no hurt.

Then was the king exceeding glad for him, and commanded that they should take Daniel up out of the den. So Daniel was taken up out of the den, and no manner of hurt was found upon him, because he believed in his God.

(Daniel 6)

David Kossoff

The first Bible story I ever attempted,
at the BBC's invitation, was Jonah, who
struck me a great character full of
everyday-met frailties of nature. I did
my version on TV and good Jonah changed
– at least added to – my life. Eventually
I wrote for radio & TV every major story
in the Old & New Testament. They became
books, records and cassettes. For a long
time Jonah (one is loyal to one's friends)
was part of one of my one-man-shows.
He pleased many audiences, my
third-division prophet!

Here, to amuse, is part of my version.

David Kossoff

Not that Jonah wanted to be a prophet. He wasn't even very good at being a prophet, and was very cross at having to be one. Mind you, some of the things that happened to Jonah would have made anybody cross.

Jonah was quite an ordinary man. Not rich; not poor. Rather inclined to argue – with anybody. Hard-headed, obstinate sort of man. Even when he received a message direct from God he argued. Suddenly, straight into Jonah's mind God had spoken. Unmistakably God; and there was no mistaking the message either. God spoke clearly. 'Jonah,' he said, 'I have an errand for you. I want you to go to Assyria, to the great city of Nineveh, and tell them that I know how wicked they've all become and that in forty days from your arrival the city wall will be destroyed and the people will perish.'

Jonah thought for a minute and then decided to argue. 'Look, God,' he said, 'Nineveh is a long way and it's not the time of year for long journeys – it's too hot. But the main point is I don't want to be made to look foolish. Look,' he said, 'you're not the kind of God that destroys cities and wipes out thousands of people. You're gracious and kind and slow to anger and merciful, and everyone knows it. I'll go all that way, make a lot of speeches and nothing will happen, and I'll look silly.'

There was a little pause and then God, who was rather used to people like Jonah said, 'Leave first thing in the morning.' And Jonah knew that he'd better shut up.

The next morning, very bad-tempered, he packed a few things together and started the long hot walk to Nineveh. He was cross when he set off and by the time he got to Jaffa he was even **more** cross.

Now the fact that Jaffa was a port gave him an idea. He said to himself, 'I won't go to Nineveh at all. I'll get a ship and go to Tarsish – in Spain. I'll hide. Who wants to be a prophet, and be made to look daft?' He found a ship that was going to Tarsish, bought his ticket and went aboard. Very silly. As he was soon to find out. He went below and very tired from his long walk he dropped into a deep sleep. The captain ordered the anchor lifted and they set sail. A hot calm day with a slight breeze. Very pleasant. Jonah slept on.

Now God, who was a little surprised at Jonah's disobedience, decided to take a hand. The skies became grey and leaden. The breeze stopped. Everything grew still and close. And then, suddenly, from nowhere, the hurricane struck! Panic was everywhere. Passengers and crew screamed and shouted and were full of fear. Jonah, below in a corner of the hold, slept on. The captain ordered everyone to pray to their various gods to find out which one was cross. Vows were made, sacrifices were promised. But of course nothing happened. The great roaring wind did not lessen one bit.

Then the captain came upon Jonah fast asleep and woke him roughly. 'Ah,' said Jonah, 'are we there?'

'**There!**' said the captain. 'The only place we're likely to be is at the bottom of the sea. Never known a storm like it. Sea's gone mad! Come on,' he said, 'up on deck. I've got everyone praying to their different gods to try and stop it. Up you go,' he said, 'get started'.

When Jonah came out on deck into the screaming wind and among the weeping, praying people, he knew at once what was up. He took the captain to one side. 'Look,' he said. 'It's my God. I'm a Hebrew and we only have one. There **is** only one. And he looks after everything. I've done something I shouldn't have – or rather I haven't done something I should have and this hurricane is all **my** fault.'

'Well,' said the captain, 'do something about it. Start praying.'

Jonah said, 'I don't think it would do any good. If I were you I'd have me tossed overboard. I've got a very strong feeling that's the only solution.'

The captain said: 'Have you tossed . . . I couldn't do a thing like that! Had my own ship thirty years and never lost a passenger yet. I can't go tossin' – it's against the regulations! Besides it may not work and in these seas I couldn't guarantee to fish you out again. Also, quite frankly, I don't really believe there **is** only one God. Seems a lot of work for just one. Try praying. I'll come back.'

But the storm grew worse and somehow the word got round among the terrified people that it was all Jonah's fault. So, when the captain came back followed by the crew and passengers, Jonah got to his feet, apologised to the captain, and allowed himself to be dropped over the side.

Immediately the sea became calm and the hurricane died away and the sun came out and the sky became blue. As Jonah floated away from the ship he could hear the captain leading prayers to the one and only God.

(Extract from 'Jonah' in **Bible Stories** by David Kossoff, published by Collins.)

Some letters without selections

Some of the people who very kindly took the trouble to reply to our letters, but who for various reasons did not select a passage from the Bible, were:

David Attenborough
Jasper Carrott
John Cleese
Big Daddy
Steve Davis
Lenny Henry
Jimmy Hill
Spike Milligan
David Williams (Manager, Bristol Rovers).

Matthew Kelly, of 'Game for a Laugh', reminded us of the Narnia stories by C.S. Lewis, **The Lion, the Witch and the Wardrobe** and **The Last Battle** (published by Lion, and a really unusual way of finding out more about the Christian faith), which he says 'my wife Sarah and I used to read to each other when she was having our first child Matthew. They are still a constant source of joy to each of us all these years later.'

British and European 'Superstars' champion, judo star Brian Jacks wrote:

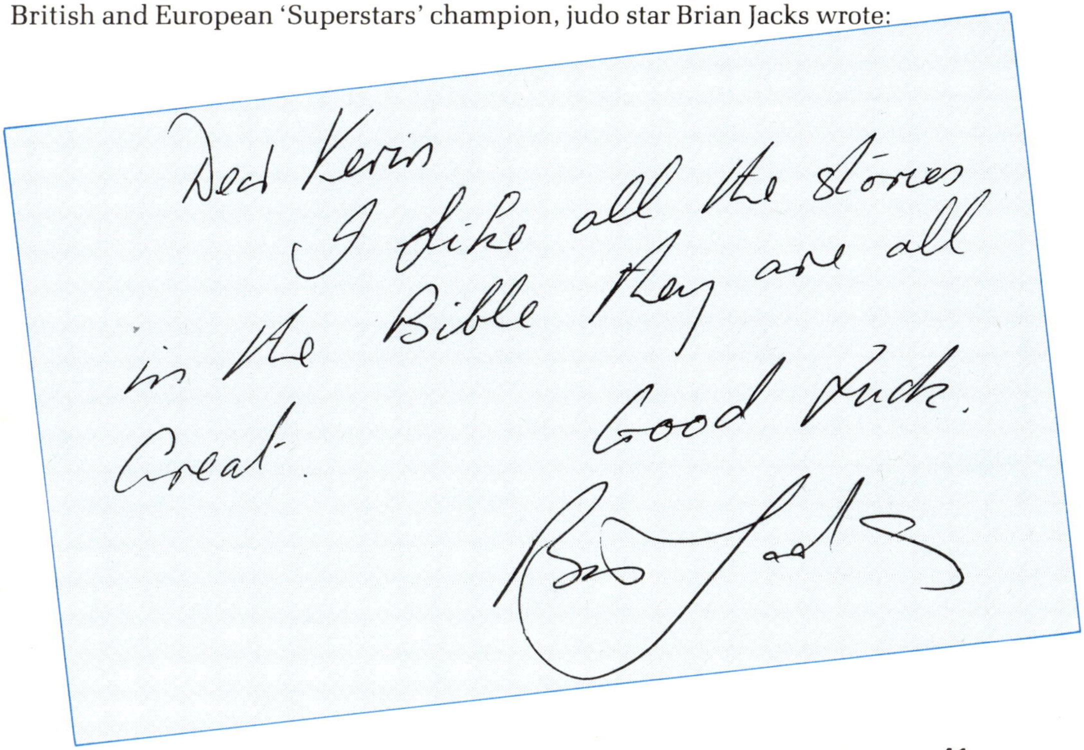
Dear Kevin
I like all the stories in the Bible they are all Great.
Good Luck.

Keith Joseph

DEPARTMENT OF EDUCATION AND SCIENCE

ELIZABETH HOUSE, YORK ROAD, LONDON SE1 7PH

TELEPHONE 01-928 9222

FROM THE SECRETARY OF STATE

Salman Bhaidani
Greenway Boys' Comprehensive School
Doncaster Road
Westbury-on-Trym
Bristol BS10 5PY

Dear Salman Bhaidani,

Thank you for your undated letter. I know that I should have answered it long ago but I live under a flood of post.

I have no photograph of myself but here is a proverb that you may like to include in your book. It is a proverb that is said to be in use both in Poland and Spain - but it seems to me to be applicable everywhere.

"Take what you like" said God "take it and pay for it."

I hope that the book goes well. Thank you for sending a stamp. I am sorry not to have replied earlier.

Yours sincerely,

Keith Joseph

Michael Foot

HOUSE OF COMMONS
LONDON SW1A 0AA

Dear Martin Hill,

I am sorry not to have replied to your letter before and I fear your teacher has set a difficult task for me to respond to properly.

Perhaps the best thing is for me to recall the words of my father who was a lay preacher in the Plymouth area. As children we would go along and listen to his sermons. He would talk on <u>Hope</u>, <u>The gospel of hope</u>. And I can assure you that we would leave the chapel much more cheerfully than we had entered it.

I don't know if this will be enough to encourage you to discuss it, but I do hope so.

All best wishes,
Yours sincerely,

Michael Foot

Mr. Martin Hill MICHAEL FOOT.

Big Daddy

Matthew Kelly

Brian Jacks

Ronnie Corbett

Ronnie Corbett

Dear Karl Butler and Michael Cudden,

Thank you very much for your letters. I'm sorry that a reply has taken so long to reach you but the letters have rather followed me all over the place and I am actually replying to you now from Southampton where we are working on our Two Ronnies stage revue prior to its coming to London. I have been rather more all over the place than Ronnie Barker has been, therefore, my reply is rather later and more dilitory. Hope I will be excused and that its not too late. I am also copping out from another of your requests, because I found it difficult, not having a copy of the Bible to hand, to select a piece that would be absolutely my favourite so I have not chosen from the Bible but have picked this poem by Robert Louis Stevenson which has connections in as much as the author is, of course, from Edinburgh and spent his childhood there. As indeed I did. I always feel that this poem contains so much love and charity that its a treasure to read and somehow particularly apposite for children. I also had the privilege of reading it at a Thanksgiving Service for the Arts in Christchurch Cathedral in New Zealand, and it always brings back thrilling

2.

memories both of New Zealand and of my childhood.

I hope you enjoy it as much as I do and I hope you don't mind my choosing this rather than the Biblical passage. It contains all the warmth and love that I think is important in such a selection.

Hope your projects go very well and that I'm excused for being so late in getting down to it.

Kind regards.

Ronnie Corbett

Enc.

Dedication
To Alison Cunningham
From her boy

For the long nights you lay awake
And watched for my unworthy sake;
For your most comfortable hand
That led me through the uneven land:
For all the story-books you read,
For all the pains you comforted,
For all you pitied, all you bore,
In sad and happy days of yore:
My second Mother, my first Wife,
The angel of my infant life-
From the sick child, now well and old,
Take, nurse, the little book you hold!

And grant it, Heaven, that all who read
May find as dear a nurse at need,
And every child who lists my rhyme,
In the bright fireside, nursery clime,
May hear it in as kind a voice
As made my childish days rejoice!

R.L.S.

Her Majesty The Queen

BUCKINGHAM PALACE

Dear Iain.

I am commanded by The Queen to write and thank you for your letter.

I have to tell you that Her Majesty and The Duke of Edinburgh do not publicise their personal preferences. I am sure you will understand that they have had to make this strict rule owing to the many hundreds of requests which they receive, and that it would be most unfair if an exception were made for one person and not for others.

Yours sincerely.

Kathryn Dugdale.

Lady-in-Waiting

Iain Aitchson,
Greenway Boys' Comprehensive School,
Doncaster Road,
Westbury-on-Trym,
Bristol BS10 5PY.

His Holiness Pope Paul II

SECRETARIAT OF STATE

FROM THE VATICAN

Dear Simon,

I have been directed to acknowledge the letter which you addressed to His Holiness Pope John Paul II. The sentiments which prompted you to write are appreciated, but I regret that it is not possible to comply with your request.

I have pleasure however in informing you that His Holiness invokes God's abundant blessings upon you and your friends.

Yours sincerely,

Mgr G.B. Re
Assessor

Simon Piper
Greenway Boys' Comprehensive School
Doncaster Road
Westbury - on - Trym
Bristol
BS10 5PY

Basil Hume

ARCHBISHOP'S HOUSE,
WESTMINSTER, LONDON, SW1P 1QJ

Dear Martin,

Thank you very much indeed for your letter.

I find it very difficult to answer your question. I often get asked to produce favourite prayers and poems and I normally refuse - quite simply because I have lots of favourites. But I am sending you a photograph.

With kindest regards.

Yours sincerely,

Archbishop of Westminster

Martin Hill,
Greenway Boys' Comprehensive School.

Lenny Henry

Jasper Carrott

John Cleese

Steve Davis

The New Testament

Harry Carpenter

BRITISH BROADCASTING CORPORATION
KENSINGTON HOUSE RICHMOND WAY LONDON W14 0AX
TELEPHONE 01-743 1272 TELEX: 265781
TELEGRAMS AND CABLES: TELECASTS LONDON TELEX

Dear Peter,

I think my favourite Bible passage remains the one from St. Matthew telling how the wise men from the east came to visit Jesus in Bethlehem: verses 9, 10 and 11 from Chapter 2:-

"When they had heard the king, they departed; and, lo, the star, which they saw in the east, went before them, till it came and stood over where the young child was.

When they saw the star, they rejoiced with exceeding great joy.

And when they were come into the house, they saw the young child with Mary his mother, and fell down, and worshipped him: and when they had opened their treasures, they presented unto him gifts; gold, and frankincense, and myrrh."

These are simple, beautiful words recounting a wonderful story. I suppose these words are my earliest recollection of the Bible and to this day they move me, perhaps because Christmas is my favourite time of the year, when my family surrounds me, and love is in the house.

Yours sincerely,

Harry Carpenter

H.R.H. Prince Charles

BUCKINGHAM PALACE

From: M.M. Colborne, Esq.

Dear Mr Hayes,

Thank you very much for your letter to The Prince of Wales. His Royal Highness has asked me to tell you that the bible passage he finds most helpful in giving him a useful direction in life, and a rule to try and operate by is in Matthew, chaper 7, verse 12 - "Therefore all things whatsoever ye would that men should do to you, do ye even so to them."

Yours sincerely

Michael Colborne

Secretary

The Archbishop of Canterbury

Lambeth Palace, SE1 7JU.

Dear Nigel,

Many thanks for your letter. One of many favourite texts in the Bible comes from the tenth chapter of St Matthew's Gospel, verse eight: 'Freely ye have received, freely give'.

When I was training to be a priest, I had a very saintly Indian friend called M A Thomas who lived in the next room. One of my clearest memories from that period is hearing him through the wall pacing up and down repeating this beautiful phrase in Greek, the original language of the New Testament, which he was then learning.

I hope that your project will be both very successful and enjoyable.

With my blessing and all good wishes,

Yours sincerely,

Nigel Thomas Esq
Greenway Boys' Comprehensive School
Doncaster Road
Westbury-On-Trym
Bristol BS10 5PY

And when he had called unto his twelve disciples, he gave them power against unclean spirits, to cast them out, and to heal all manner of sickness and all manner of disease.

Now the names of the twelve apostles are these; The first, Simon, who is called Peter, and Andrew his brother; James the son of Zebedee, and John his brother;

Philip, and Bartholomew; Thomas, and Matthew the publican; James the son of Alphaeus, and Lebbaeus, whose surname was Thaddaeus;

Simon the Canaanite, and Judas Iscariot, who also betrayed him.

These twelve Jesus sent forth, and commanded them, saying, Go not into the way of the Gentiles, and into any city of the Samaritans enter ye not:

But go rather to the lost sheep of the house of Israel.

And as ye go, preach, saying, The kingdom of heaven is at hand.

Heal the sick, cleanse the lepers, raise the dead, cast out devils: freely ye have received, freely give.

Provide neither gold, nor silver, nor brass in your purses,

Nor scrip for your journey, neither two coats, neither shoes, nor yet staves: for the workman is worthy of his meat.

(Matthew 10. 1 – 10)

Ronnie Barker

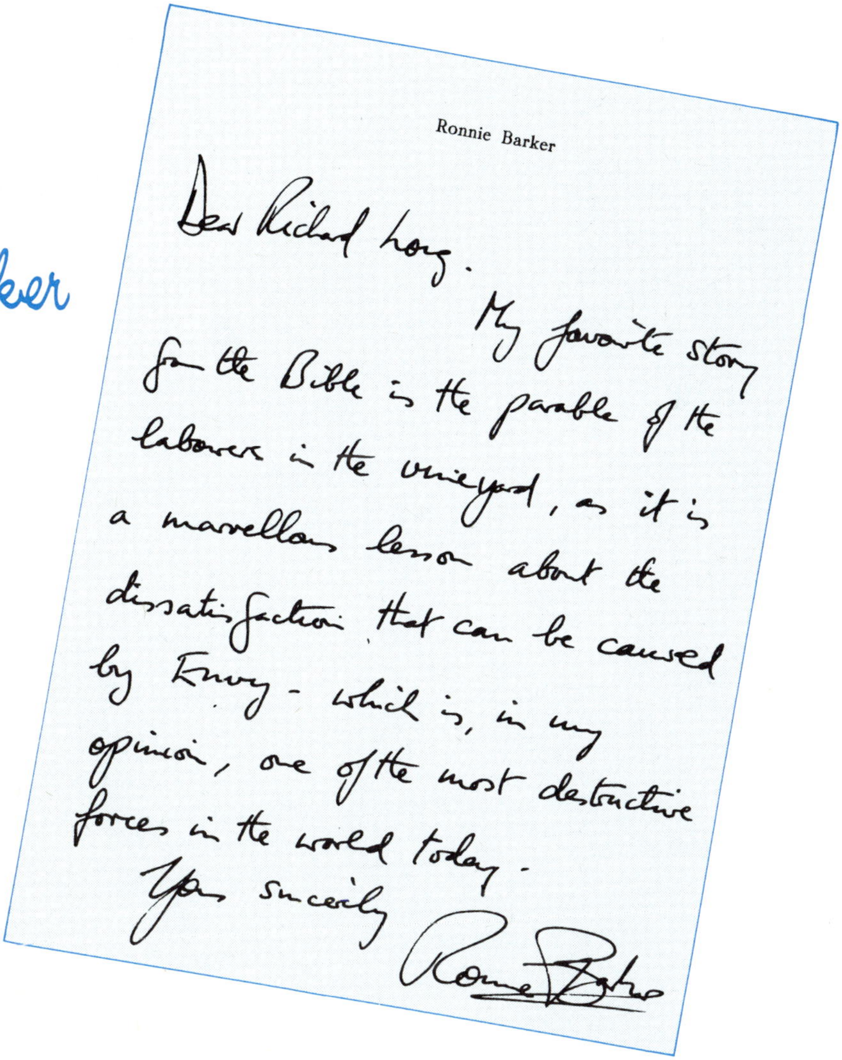

Ronnie Barker

Dear Richard Long.

My favourite story from the Bible is the parable of the labourers in the vineyard, as it is a marvellous lesson about the dissatisfaction that can be caused by Envy - which is, in my opinion, one of the most destructive forces in the world today.

Yours sincerely

Ronnie Barker

(Jesus said:)

"The Kingdom of heaven is like this. Once there was a man who went out early in the morning to hire some men to work in his vineyard. He agreed to pay them the regular wage, a silver coin a day, and sent them to work in his vineyard. He went out again to the market place at nine o'clock and saw some men standing there doing nothing, so he told them, 'You also go and work in the vineyard, and I will pay you a fair wage.' So they went. Then at twelve o'clock and again at three o'clock he did the same thing. It was nearly five o'clock when he went to the market place and saw some other men still standing there. 'Why are you wasting the whole day here doing nothing?' he asked them. 'No one hired us,' they answered. 'Well, then, you also go and work in the vineyard,' he told them.

"When evening came, the owner told his foreman, 'Call the workers and pay them their wages, starting with those who were hired last and ending with those who were hired first.' The men who had begun to work at five were paid a silver coin each. So when the men who were the first to be hired came to be paid, they thought they would get more; but they too were given a silver coin each. They took their money and started grumbling against the employer. 'These men who were hired last worked only one hour,' they said, 'while we put up with a whole day's work in the hot sun – yet you paid them the same as you paid us!'

'Listen, friend,' the owner answered one of them, 'I have not cheated you. After all, you agreed to do a day's work for one silver coin. Now take your pay and go home. I want to give this man who was hired last as much as I have given you. Don't I have the right to do as I wish with my own money? Or are you jealous because I am generous?' "

And Jesus concluded, "So those who are last will be first, and those who are first will be last."

(Matthew 20. 1 – 16. Good News Bible)

Bruce Hockin

For the kingdom of heaven is as a man travelling into a far country, who called his own servants, and delivered unto them his goods.

And unto one he gave five talents, to another two, and to another one; to every man according to his several ability; and straightway took his journey. Then he that had received the five talents went out and traded with the same, and made them another five talents.

And likewise he that had received two, he also gained two.

But he that had received one, went and digged in the earth, and hid his lord's money.

After a long time, the lord of those servants cometh, and reckoneth with them. And so he that had received five talents came and brought other five talents, saying, Lord, thou deliveredst unto me five talents: behold, I have gained beside them five talents more.

His lord said unto him, Well done, thou good and faithful servant: thou hast been faithful over a few things, I will make thee ruler over many things: enter thou into the joy of thy lord.

He also that had received two talents came and said, Lord thou deliveredst unto me two talents: behold, I have gained two other talents beside them. His lord said unto him, Well done, good and faithful servant; thou hast been faithful over a few things, I will make thee ruler over many things: enter thou into the joy of thy lord.

Then he which had received the one talent came and said, Lord I knew thee that thou art an hard man, reaping where thou hast not sown, and gathering where thou hast not strawed:

And I was afraid, and went and hid thy talent in the earth: lo, there thou hast that is thine.

His lord answered and said unto him, Thou wicked and slothful servant, thou knewest that I reap where I sowed not, and gather where I have not strawed: Thou oughtest therefore to have put my money to the exchangers, and then at my coming I should have received mine own with usury.

Take therefore the talent from him, and give it unto him which hath ten talents. For unto every one that hath shall be given, and he shall have abundance: but from him that hath not shall be taken away even that which he hath.

(Matthew 25. 14 – 29)

HTV WEST

HTV LIMITED THE TELEVISION CENTRE BRISTOL BS4 3HG TELEPHONE 0272 778366 TELEX 44156

BH/DB

Martin Hill,
Avon Education Service,
Greenway Boys' Comprehensive School,
Doncaster Road,
Westbury-on-Trym,
BRISTOL.
BS10 5PY

Dear Martin,

Thank you for your letter. I was most interested to hear about your project and, of course, I am only too willing to assist you. My favourite passage from the Bible is the story of the talents which is found in St. Matthew's Gospel chapter 25, verses 14 to 29. In this, I think, is a message for all of us to make the best possible use of what we have. Since my school-days I have so often been reminded about this parable .

You asked for a photograph. I am enclosing one for your project and one for you personally and I do hope that everything works out well with your book.

Yours sincerely,

BRUCE HOCKIN

Frankie Howerd

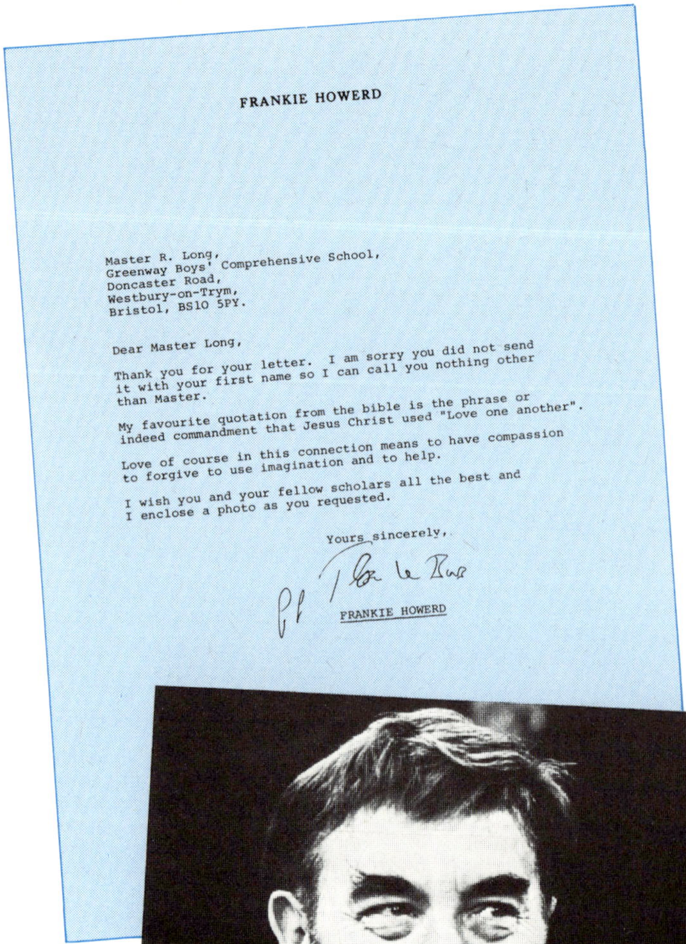

FRANKIE HOWERD

Master R. Long,
Greenway Boys' Comprehensive School,
Doncaster Road,
Westbury-on-Trym,
Bristol, BS10 5PY.

Dear Master Long,

Thank you for your letter. I am sorry you did not send it with your first name so I can call you nothing other than Master.

My favourite quotation from the bible is the phrase or indeed commandment that Jesus Christ used "Love one another".

Love of course in this connection means to have compassion to forgive to use imagination and to help.

I wish you and your fellow scholars all the best and I enclose a photo as you requested.

Yours sincerely,

FRANKIE HOWERD

A teacher of the Law was there who heard the discussion. He saw that Jesus had given the Sadducees a good answer, so he came to him with a question: "Which commandment is the most important of all?"

Jesus replied, "The most important one is this, 'Listen, Israel! The Lord our God is the only Lord. Love the Lord your God with all your heart, with all your soul, with all your mind, and with all your strength.' The second most important commandment is this: 'Love your neighbour as you love yourself.' There is no other commandment more important than these two."

The teacher of the Law said to Jesus, "Well done, Teacher! It is true, as you say, that only the Lord is God and that there is no other god but he. And man must love God with all his heart and with all his mind and with all his strength; and he must love his neighbour as he loves himself. It is more important to obey these two commandments than to offer animals and other sacrifices to God."

Jesus noticed how wise his answer was, and so he told him, "You are not far from the Kingdom of God."

After this nobody dared to ask Jesus any more questions.

(Mark 12, 28 – 34. Good News Bible)

Jane Rossington

Central Independent Television plc
Central House
Broad Street
Birmingham B1 2JP

CENTRAL

Telephone 021-643 9898
Telex 338966
Cables and telegrams:
Television Birmingham

Dear Dee,

Thank you for your interesting letter – now my favourite Bible story has got to be the Christmas story – really because of my children who are deep into it. I love Christmas and everything to do with it.

Yours sincerely,

Jane Rossington

Directors: Cliff Baty, Ellis Birk, Charles Denton, John Jackson, David Justham, John Madocks CBE DL, Peter Mears, Jean Parker, Sir David Perris MBE JP, Sir Leo Pliatzky KCB, Murray Thomson
Sir Gordon Hobday (Chairman), Robert Phillis (Managing Director)
Colin Campbell (Secretary) Registered Office: Central House, Broad Street, Birmingham B1 2JP. Registered in England and Wales, No. 1490357

And it came to pass in those days that there went out a decree from Caesar Augustus, that all the world should be taxed.

(And this taxing was first made when Cyrenius was governor of Syria.) And all went to be taxed, every one into his own city.

And Joseph also went up from Galilee, out of the city of Nazareth, into Judaea, unto the city of David, which is called Bethlehem; (because he was of the house and lineage of David:)

To be taxed with Mary his espoused wife, being great with child. And so it was that, while they were there, the days were accomplished that she should be delivered.

And she brought forth her firstborn son, and wrapped him in swaddling clothes, and laid him in a manger; because there was no room for them in the inn.

And there were in the same country shepherds abiding in the field, keeping watch over their flock by night.

And, lo, the angel of the Lord came upon them, and the glory of the Lord shone round about them: and they were sore afraid.

And the angel said unto them, Fear not: for, behold, I bring you tidings of great joy, which shall be to all people.

For unto you is born this day in the city of David a Saviour, which is Christ the Lord.

And this shall be a sign unto you; Ye shall find the babe wrapped in swaddling clothes, lying in a manger.

And suddenly there was with the angel a multitude of the heavenly host praising God and saying,

Glory to God in the highest, and on earth peace, good will toward men.

And it came to pass, as the angels were gone away from them into heaven, the shepherds said to one another, Let us now go even unto Bethlehem, and see this thing which is come to pass, which the Lord hath made known unto us.

And they came with haste, and found Mary, and Joseph, and the babe lying in a manger.

And when they had seen it, they made known abroad the saying which was told them concerning this child.

And all they that heard it wondered at those things which were told them by the shepherds.

But Mary kept all these things, and pondered them in her heart. And the shepherds returned, glorifying and praising God for all the things they had heard and seen, as it was told unto them.

(Luke 2. 1 – 20)

Benny Hill

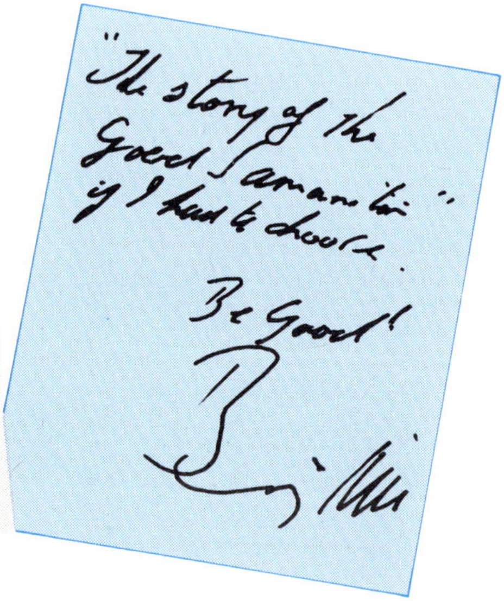

Tony Benn

And, behold, a certain lawyer stood up, and tempted him, saying, Master, what shall I do to inherit eternal life?

He said to him, What is written in the law? How readest thou?

And he answering said, Thou shalt love the Lord thy God with all thy heart, and with all thy soul, and with all thy strength, and with all thy mind; and thy neighbour as thyself.

And he said unto him, Thou hast answered right: this do, and thou shalt live. But he, willing to justify himself, said unto Jesus, And who is my neighbour?

And Jesus answering said, A certain man went down from Jerusalem to Jericho, and fell among thieves, which stripped him of his raiment, and wounded him, and departed, leaving him half dead.

And by chance there came down a certain priest that way: and when he saw him, he passed by on the other side.

And likewise a Levite, when he was at the place, came and looked on him, and passed by on the other side.

But a certain Samaritan, as he journeyed, came where he was: and when he saw him, he had compassion on him,

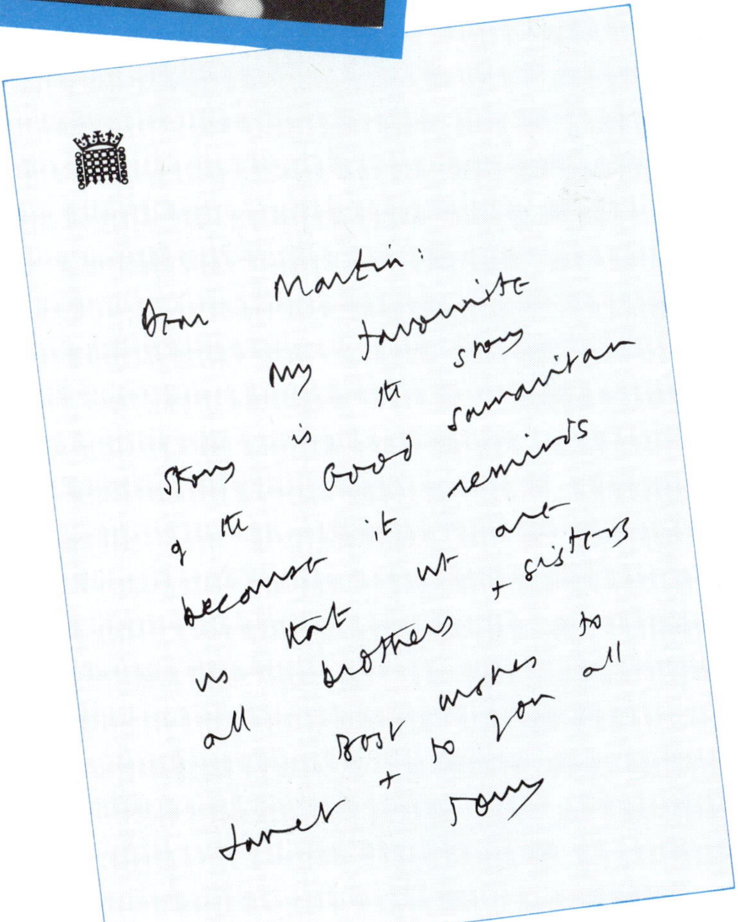

Dear Martin:

My favourite story is the story of the Good Samaritan because it reminds us that we are all brothers + sisters

Best wishes to Janet + to you all

Tony

Terry Cooper

And went to him, and bound up his wounds, pouring in oil and wine, and set him on his own beast, and brought him to an inn, and took care of him.

And on the morrow when he departed, he took out two pence, and gave them to the host, and said unto him, Take care of him; and whatsoever thou spendest more, when I come again, I will repay thee.

Which now of these three, thinkest thou, was neighbour unto him that fell among the thieves?

And he said, He that shewed mercy on him. Then said Jesus unto him, Go, and do thou likewise.

(Luke 10. 25 – 37)

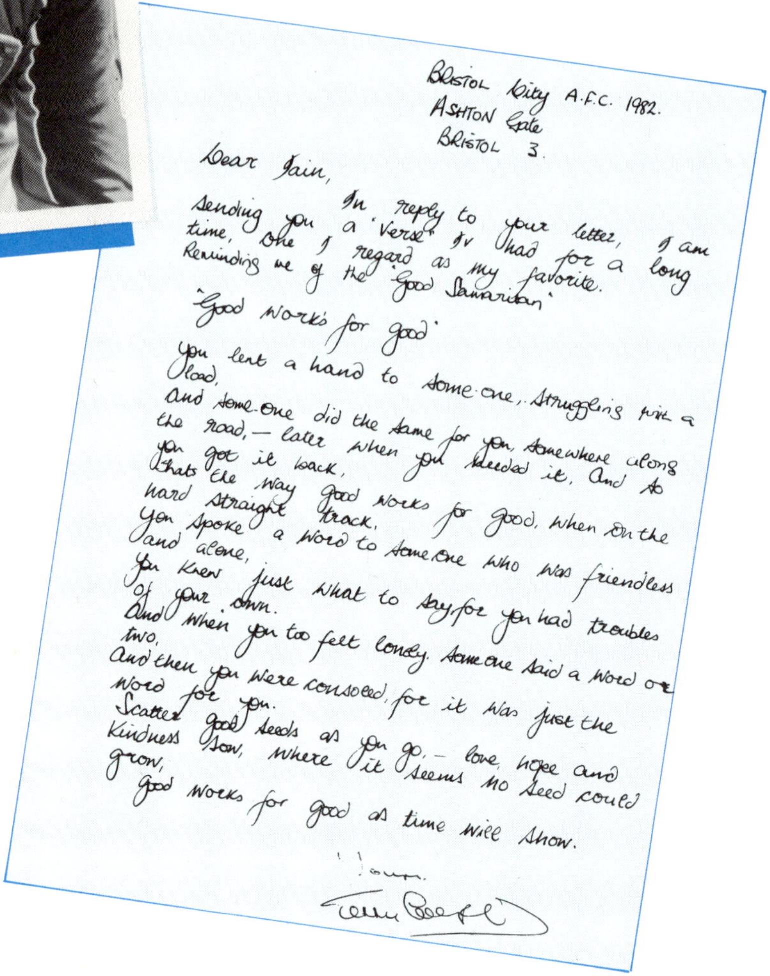

Bristol City A.F.C. 1982.
Ashton Gate
Bristol 3.

Dear Iain,

In reply to your letter, I am sending you a 'Verse' I've had for a long time, one I regard as my favorite. Reminding me of the 'Good Samaritan'.

"Good Works for good"

You lent a hand to some-one, struggling with a load,
And some-one did the same for you, somewhere along the road, — later when you needed it, And so you got it back,
Thats the way good works for good, when on the hard straight track,
You spoke a word to some-one who was friendless and alone,
You knew just what to say, for you had troubles of your own.
And when you too felt lonely, some one said a word or two,
And then you were consoled, for it was just the word for you.
Scatter good seeds as you go, — love, hope and kindness sow, where it seems no seed could grow,
Good works for good as time will show.

Ruth Madoc

RUTH MADOC

(Personal Manager JOHN JACKSON)

The Hippodrome Theatre
Bristol.

Dear Iain,

I was pleased to receive your letter asking me for my favourite Bible verse or "Story".

Well, after great thought, I think my favourite story is probably the parable of the "lost sheep & the. of the prodigal son" taken from "St Luke". Chapter 15. My favourite verse or quotation is "Ask, and it shall be given you; seek, and ye shall find, knock, and it shall be opened unto you", St Matthew, chapter 7, verse, 7.

I like to wish you every success with the book; and my kindest regards to your friends & pupils of the school.

Yours sincerely

Ruth Madoc.

One day when many tax collectors and other outcasts came to listen to Jesus, the Pharisees and the teachers of the Law started grumbling, "This man welcomes outcasts and even eats with them!" So Jesus told them this parable:

"Suppose one of you has a hundred sheep and loses one of them – what does he do? He leaves the other ninety-nine sheep in the pasture and goes looking for the one that got lost until he finds it. When he finds it, he is so happy that he puts it on his shoulders and carries it back home.

Then he calls his friends and neighbours together and says to them, 'I am so happy I found my lost sheep. Let us celebrate!' In the same way, I tell you, there will be more joy in heaven over one sinner who repents than over ninety-nine respectable people who do not need to repent . . .''

Jesus went on to say, ''There was once a man who had two sons. The younger said to him, 'Father, give me my share of the property now.' So the man divided his property between his two sons. After a few days the younger son sold his part of the property and left home with the money. He went to a country far away, where he wasted his money in reckless living. He spent everything he had. Then a severe famine spread over that country, and he was left without a thing. So he went to work for one of the citizens of that country, who sent him out to his farm to take care of the pigs. He wished he could fill himself with the bean pods the pigs ate, but no one gave him anything to eat. At last he came to his senses and said, 'All my father's hired workers have more than they can eat, and here I am about to starve! I will get up and go to my father and say, Father, I have sinned against God and against you. I am no longer fit to be called your son; treat me as one of your hired workers.' So he got up and started back to his father.

''He was still a long way from home when his father saw him; his heart was filled with pity, and he ran, threw his arms round his son, and kissed him. 'Father,' the son said, 'I have sinned against God and against you. I am no longer fit to be called your son.' But the father called his servants. 'Hurry!' he said. 'Bring the best robe and put it on him. Put a ring on his finger and shoes on his feet. Then go and get the prize calf and kill it, and let us celebrate with a feast! For this son of mine was dead, but now he is alive; he was lost, but now he has been found.' And so the feasting began.

''In the meantime the elder son was out in the field. On his way back, when he came close to the house, he heard the music and dancing. So he called one of the servants and asked him, 'What's going on?' 'Your brother has come back home,' the servant answered, 'and your father has killed the prize calf because he got him back safe and sound.'

''The elder brother was so angry that he would not go into the house; so his father came out and begged him to come in. But he answered his father, 'Look, all these years I have worked for you like a slave, and I have never disobeyed your orders. What have you given me? Not even a goat for me to have a feast with my friends! But this son of yours wasted all your property on prostitutes, and when he comes back home, you kill the prize calf for him!' 'My son,' the father answered, 'you are always here with me, and everything I have is yours. But we had to celebrate and be happy, because your brother was dead, but now he is alive; he was lost, but now he has been found.' ''

(Luke 15. 1 – 7, 1 – 32. Good News Bible)

Sandor Elès

(Jesus said:)

The kingdom of God cometh not with observation: Neither shall they say, Lo here! or lo there! for behold, the kingdom of God is within you.

(Luke 17. 20, 21)

(Jesus said:)

My sheep hear my voice and I know them, and they follow me;

And I give unto them eternal life; and they shall never perish, neither shall any man pluck them out of my hand.

My Father, which gave them me, is greater than all; and no man is able to pluck them out of my Father's hand.

I and my Father are one.

(John 10. 27 – 30)

Arthur Scargill

NATIONAL UNION OF MINEWORKERS

ST. JAMES' HOUSE, VICAR LANE,
SHEFFIELD, SOUTH YORKSHIRE S1 2EX

Secretary L. DALY

President A. SCARGILL *Telephone:* 0742 700388

Please quote our reference in reply:

Your Ref:

Our Ref: N.O. 23/HC/JB

Master J. Long,
c/o Greenway Boys' Comprehensive,
Doncaster Road,
Westbury on Trym,
Bristol.
BS10 5PY

Dear Master Long,

Thank you for your letter. My favourite passage in the Bible is the one of Jesus turning the money lenders out of the temple because he objected to their making profits out of other peoples religious beliefs.

I hope that this information will be useful to you.

Yours sincerely,

A. Scargill
President

'Our Headmaster' Mr. Godfrey

And the Jews' passover was at hand, and Jesus went up to Jerusalem,

And found in the temple those that sold oxen and sheep and doves, and the changers of money sitting:

And when he had made a scourge of small cords, he drove them all out of the temple, and the sheep, and the oxen; and poured out the changers' money, and overthrew the tables;

And said unto them that sold doves, Take these things hence; make not my Father's house an house of merchandise.

And his disciples remembered that it was written, The zeal of thine house hath eaten me up.

(John 2. 13 – 17)

AVON EDUCATION SERVICE

GREENWAY BOYS' COMPREHENSIVE SCHOOL
DONCASTER ROAD
WESTBURY-ON-TRYM
BRISTOL BS10 5PY
Telephone Nos. 506990 and 505885

P. B. GODFREY
Headmaster

Dear Mark,

Thank you for your letter. You have set me a very difficult task because there are so many verses and stories in the Bible that are worth reading. One that I like is in the Gospel according to St John, Chapter 2 verses 14 to 16. I strongly feel that respect must always be paid to the house of God, whether it be a church, chapel, mosque or synagogue, whether it is of any faith whatsoever; no one should despise another's religious beliefs. In fact, one of the most important things for a person to have is tolerance. So many bad happenings in the world have been due to a lack of tolerance.

I hope this partly answers your letter.

Yours sincerely,

P.B.Godfrey,
Headmaster.

Mark Potter,
Greenway Boys School,
Doncaster Road,
Southmead,
Bristol.

Ray Reardon

Gloucester Golf
& Country Hotel.

Dear Geoffrey, Many thanks for your very nice letter. I think it is a very good idea too belong to a writing group and indeed writing to famous personalities. I enclose my following passage from the bible and feel proud to have been asked.

Earlier this year my dear father Ben Reardon passed away. It was a very hard blow as he was a good man.

The passage that helped me
ST. PAUL (BOOK of Romans
Ch8. v 18.

All the Very Best
& Sincere Regards
Ray Reardon

For I reckon that the sufferings of this present time are not worthy to be compared with the glory which shall be revealed in us.

For the earnest expectation of the creature waiteth for the manifestation of the sons of God.

For the creature was made subject to vanity, not willingly, but by reason of him who hath subjected the same in hope.

Because the creature itself also shall be delivered from the bondage of corruption into the glorious liberty of the children of God.

For we know that the whole creation groaneth and travaileth in pain together until now.

And not only they, but ourselves also, which have the first fruits of the Spirit, even we ourselves groan within ourselves, waiting for the adoption, to wit, the redemption of our body.

For we are saved by hope: but hope that is seen is not hope: for what a man seeth, why doth he yet hope for?

But if we hope for that we see not, then do we with patience wait for it.

(Romans 8. 18 – 25)

Jean Rook

DAILY EXPRESS

Express
Newspapers
Limited

121 Fleet Street
London EC4P 4JT

Telephone
01-353 8000
Telex No 21841
Cable Address
Express London

Master Martin Hill
Greenway Boys' Comprehensive School
Doncaster Road
Westbury-on-Trym
BRISTOL
BS10 5PY

Dear Martin Hill

Thank you very much for your letter and for honouring me by including me in your project.

Undoubtedly my favourite passage, which I think comes from Corinthians (you may correct me here) is the one which ends:

> "Faith, hope and love, these three; but the greatest of these is love."

You may be too young to remember, but the old version read:

> "Faith, hope and charity, these three; but the greatest of these is charity."

I have chosen this because the Speaker of the House of Commons, Thomas George Thomas, read it at the wedding of the Prince and Princess of Wales, which I covered for my paper. At the moment in St. Pauls, and later listening to his wonderful Welsh voice on television I was tremendously moved to hear the passage which I have always admired being so beautifully put across.

I do hope this is of some help and forgive me for not looking up the exact location of the passage, but you catch me just back from abroad and just on my way again, so I know you won't mind looking it up for me.

Yours sincerely

Jean Rook
Assistant Editor

Registered in London No 141748. Registered office: 121 Fleet Street London EC4P 4JT

Roger Moore

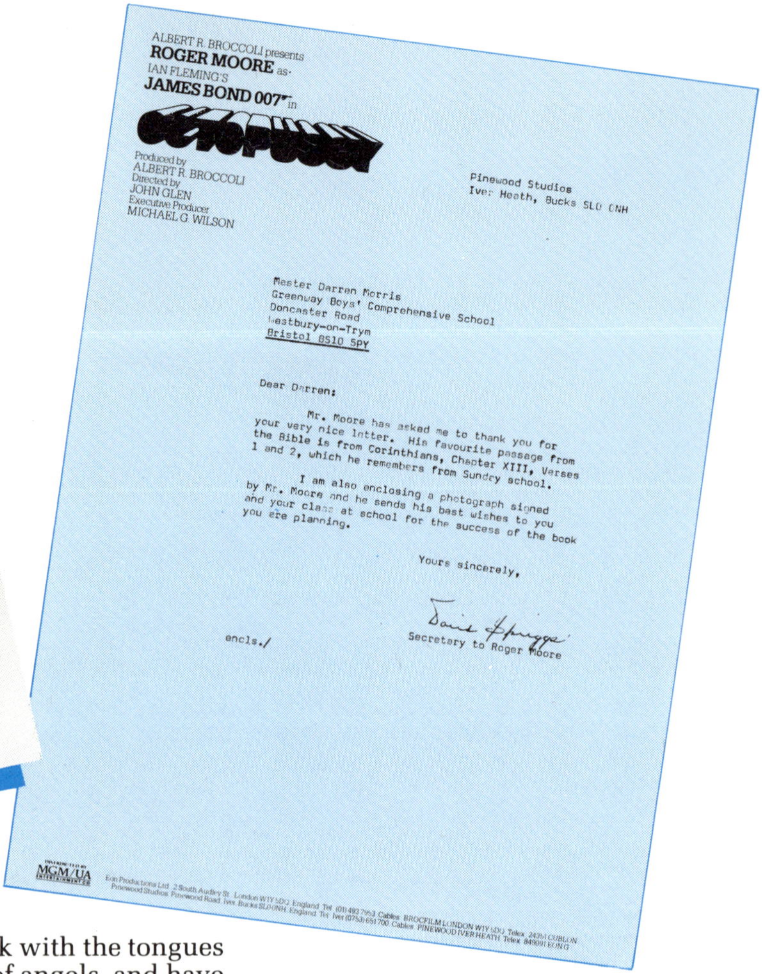

ALBERT R. BROCCOLI presents
ROGER MOORE as
IAN FLEMING'S
JAMES BOND 007™ in
OCTOPUSSY

Produced by
ALBERT R. BROCCOLI
Directed by
JOHN GLEN
Executive Producer
MICHAEL G. WILSON

Pinewood Studios
Iver Heath, Bucks SL0 0NH

Master Darren Morris
Greenway Boys' Comprehensive School
Doncaster Road
Westbury-on-Trym
Bristol BS10 5PY

Dear Darren:

Mr. Moore has asked me to thank you for your very nice letter. His favourite passage from the Bible is from Corinthians, Chapter XIII, Verses 1 and 2, which he remembers from Sunday school.

I am also enclosing a photograph signed by Mr. Moore and he sends his best wishes to you and your class at school for the success of the book you are planning.

Yours sincerely,

Secretary to Roger Moore

encls./

DISTRIBUTED BY MGM/UA ENTERTAINMENT CO.

Eon Productions Ltd. 2 South Audley St. London W1Y 5DQ England Tel. (01) 493 7953 Cables: BROCFILM LONDON W1Y 5DQ Telex 23451 CUBLON
Pinewood Studios Pinewood Road Iver Bucks SL0 0NH England Tel. Iver (0753) 651 700 Cables: PINEWOOD IVER HEATH Telex 849091 EON G

Though I speak with the tongues of men and of angels, and have not charity, I am become as sounding brass, or a tinkling cymbal.

And though I have the gift of prophecy, and understand all mysteries, and all knowledge; and though I have all faith, so that I could remove mountains, and have not charity, I am nothing.

And though I bestow all my goods to feed the poor, and though I give my body to be burned, and have not charity, it profiteth me nothing.

Charity suffereth long, and is kind; charity envieth not; charity vaunteth not itself, is not puffed up,

Doth not behave itself unseemly, seeketh not her own, is not easily provoked, thinketh no evil;

Rejoiceth not in iniquity, but rejoiceth in the truth;

Beareth all things, believeth all things, hopeth all things, endureth all things.

Charity never faileth: but whether there be prophecies, they shall fail; whether there be tongues, they shall cease; whether there be knowledge, it shall vanish away.

For we know in part, and we prophesy in part.

But when that which is perfect is come, then that which is in part shall be done away.

When I was a child, I spake as a child, I understood as a child, I thought as a child: but when I became a man, I put away childish things.

For now we see through a glass, darkly; but then face to face: now I know in part; but then shall I know even as also I am known.

And now abideth faith, hope, charity, these three; but the greatest of these is charity.

(I Corinthians 13)

Cliff Richard

Cliff Richard

HARLEY HOUSE SOUTH · PORTSMOUTH ROAD · ESHER · SURREY · KT10 9BH
TELEPHONE: ESHER 65702

GS/S

Mr Lee Williams
Greenway Boys' Comprehensive School
Doncaster Road
Westbury-on-Trym
Bristol, BS10 5PY

Dear Lee

Thank you for your letter to Cliff Richard, on whose behalf I reply.

Cliff's very busy schedule doesn't allow him to reply personally, but he has asked me to say that his favourite Bible verse is: Philippians 4:13 - 'I can do all things through Christ, who strengthens me'. He thinks this is self-explanatory!

Yours sincerely

Gillian Snow (Miss)

I can do all things through Christ which strengtheneth me.

(Philippians 4. 13)

George Cole

Theatre Royal,
Drury Lane,
London, W.C.2.

Dear Mark and Lissette,

I'm afraid I'm not much of a bible man myself, so I can't really help you. I do remember a text on the wall of some terrible digs that I stayed at once. They were awful and the food was dreadful. On the wall was a text done in pokerwork. It said,'Jesus Christ the same today and everyday.'

Yours sincerely,

George Cole.

Jesus Christ the same yesterday, and today, and for ever.

(Hebrews 13. 8)

Penelope Keith

But do not forget one thing, my dear friends! There is no difference in the Lord's sight between one day and a thousand years; to him the two are the same. The Lord is not slow to do what he has promised, as some think. Instead, he is patient with you, because he does not want anyone to be destroyed, but wants all to turn away from their sins.

But the day of the Lord will come like a thief. On that Day the heavens will disappear with a shrill noise, the heavenly bodies will burn up and be destroyed, and the earth with everything in it will vanish. Since all these things will be destroyed in this way, what kind of people should you be? Your lives should be holy and dedicated to God, as you wait for the Day of God and do your best to make it come soon – the Day when the heavens will burn up and be destroyed, and the heavenly bodies will be melted by the heat. But we wait for what God has promised: new heavens and a new earth, where righteousness will be at home.

And so, my friends, as you wait for that Day, do your best to be pure and faultless in God's sight and to be at peace with him. Look on our Lord's patience as the opportunity he is giving you to be saved, just as our dear brother Paul wrote to you, using the wisdom that God gave him. This is what he says in all his letters when he writes on the subject. There are some difficult things in his letters which ignorant and unstable people explain falsely, as they do with other passages of the Scriptures. So they bring on their own destruction.

But you, my friends, already know this. Be on your guard, then, so that you will not be led away by the errors of lawless people and fall from your safe position. But continue to grow in the grace and knowledge of our Lord and Saviour Jesus Christ. To him be the glory, now and for ever! Amen.

(II Peter 3. 8 – 17. Good News Bible)

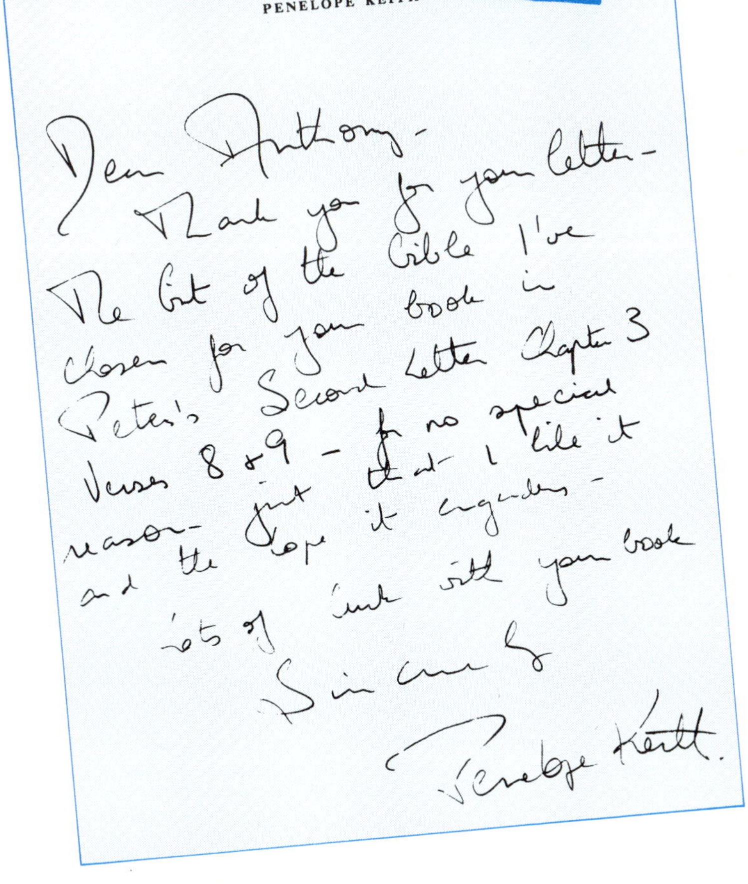

PENELOPE KEITH

Dear Anthony -
Thank you for your letter -
The bit of the Bible I've chosen for your book is Peter's Second Letter Chapter 3 Verses 8 + 9 - for no special reason - just that I like it and the hope it engenders -

lots of luck with your book

Sincerely

Penelope Keith.

Julie Goodyear

(The beginning of a letter written by 'the Elder', or senior church member, probably to a local church and its people, whom he pictures as a 'lady' with her 'children'.)

The elder unto the elect lady and her children, whom I love in the truth; and not I only, but also all they that have known the truth;

For the truth's sake, which dwelleth in us, and shall be with us for ever.

Grace be with you, mercy, and peace, from God the Father, and from the Lord Jesus Christ, the Son of the Father, in truth and love.

(II John. 1 – 3)

s J.Goodyear.
Lynch
Coronation Street
da TV
ster.

Dear Steven,

Many thanks for your letter telling me how much you enjoy Coronation Street and about your book called 'Best Bible Bits'.

Miss Goodyear has enclosed a snip from the Bible to help you with your book,she is also thrilled that you like the show and hopes that you have many more happy hours viewing.

She has also enclosed a signed photograph especially for you with her love and best wishes for the future.

Yours sincerely
Miss J.Ross
Secretary

Peter Cushing

PETER CUSHING

Dear Master Long,

Thank you for your recent letter, and for asking me to contribute a quotation for your most worthy cause. Here it is:

".....and God shall wipe away all tears from their eyes; and there shall be no more death, neither sorrow nor crying, neither shall there be any more pain; for the former things are passed away...."

(The Revelation of St. John the Divine - xxi 4)

I have chosen the above from the Bible because it gives sure hope and a certain comfort to all those who - like myself - are parted temporarily from their loved ones, and long for the promised reunion in the world to come.

Wishing you every success with your publication. May God guide your every endeavour, and His blessing be with you always.

In all sincerity,

Peter Cushing

(Enclosed is a photograph as requested)

Mrs. Ainger (a Greenway boy's mum)

And I saw a new heaven and a new earth: for the first heaven and the first earth were passed away; and there was no more sea.

And I John saw the holy city, new Jerusalem, coming down from God out of heaven, prepared as a bride adorned for her husband.

And I heard a great voice out of heaven saying, Behold, the tabernacle of God is with men, and he will dwell with them, and they shall be his people, and God himself shall be with them, and be their God.

And God shall wipe away all tears from their eyes; and there shall be no more death, neither sorrow, nor crying, neither shall there be any more pain: for the former things are passed away.

And he that sat upon the throne said, Behold, I make all things new. And he said unto me, Write: for these words are true and faithful.

(Revelation 21. 1 – 5)

Street Survey

Aim: to find out more about people's attitude to the Bible.

The boys interviewed thirty-five people.

Twenty-eight had a Bible in the house.

When asked when they last read the Bible, nine said never, thirteen couldn't remember and one had looked at it once. Five had read it last Sunday, one last month, three last year and for three it had been longer; in fact, one man stipulated a particular occasion eight years previously.

Fourteen couldn't name a favourite verse or story. Twelve mentioned Samson and Delilah, three Mark's Gospel and two the Crucifixion. The others referred to Luke's Gospel, Jonah, John and the story of Jesus lost in the Temple.

Photographic Credits . . .

Front Cover:

Ronnie Barker: BBC; HRH Prince Charles: Peter Grugeon/Camera Press London; Wendy Craig: BBC; Neil Kinnock: Andrew Wiard (Report); Esther Rantzen: BBC; Rt Hon. Margaret Thatcher MP: Conservative Central Office.

19: London Weekend Television. 31: BBC. 32: Chris Capstick. 43: Monitor Press Features Limited. 54: BBC. 55: Snowdon/Camera Press London. 58: BBC. 63: Judah Passow/ Network. 67: Sunday Times. 69: Michael Gazzard. 71: Daily Express. 74: Thames Television. 78: Andrew Beese. 79: Michael Gazzard.